The THREE PILLARS
of
EFFECTIVE
TECHNICAL
LEADERSHIP

The THREE PILLARS
of
EFFECTIVE
TECHNICAL
LEADERSHIP

Practices & Methods

Mesut Ayata

Foreword by Erik Doernenburg

The Three Pillars of Effective Technical Leadership
by Mesut Ayata

This version was published on amazon
in August, 2024

ISBN: 9798334766150

For more information: info@ayata.tech

Praise for
The Three Pillars of
Effective Technical Leadership

"The Three Pillars of Effective Technical Leadership provides both a great introduction to as well as an easy to use and comprehensive framework for technical leadership. Based on research and well established books on high performing teams it guides the reader to the most important aspects of technical leadership. At every step it provides not only clear definitions but suitable activities to improve individual aspects of a team and makes them more approachable by providing pragmatic tips.

This makes it a resource I wish I had available on my own leadership journey and a clear recommendation for both aspiring and experienced Tech Leads."

Felix Holzäpfel-Stein, Tech Lead

"Mesut has put together a set of tried & tested tools and techniques that will help Tech Leads to identify and tackle the unique set of challenges they will face!"

Kapil Dube, Tech Principal

*I dedicate my first book to my mom
who did not have a chance to go to school
and all the women in similar situations
around the world.*

Contents

FOREWORD   XV
Acknowledgements   XIX
About The Author   XXI
Audience   XXIII
Introduction   1
Effective Teams   4
Effective Technical Leadership   17
The Three Pillars   19
First Pillar: Leadership   **29**
   Building Trust: 5 Golden Rules   29
   Creating a Safe Environment   41
   Enabling, Empowering and
   Delegation   43
   Letting Your Team Members Shine   46
   Driving Challenging Technical
   Discussions   47
   1on1s   51
   Feedback Culture   54
   Reading Between Lines   59
   Team Health Checks   62
   Roles and Responsibilities   65
   Core Values and Ways of Working   70
   Onboarding / Offboarding   74
   Knowledge Distribution   76
   Tech Huddles: Why, What and How   79
   Organizing Your Day: Simple Tips 85

Summary	87
Second Pillar: Technical Excellence	**91**
What is Technical Excellence?	93
Pair Programming	95
Following New Technologies	99
Testing: Why It Matters	101
Trunk Based Development	106
System Monitoring	109
Technical Debt	112
Architecture Decision Records	116
Security and Threat Modeling	118
Preparation for Failures: Chaos Engineering	123
Continuous Delivery	126
Summary	132
Third Pillar: Value	**137**
Understanding the Value and Strategic Goals	140
Working with a Product Owner	142
Continuous Product Discovery	145
Planning & Prioritisation	147
Definitions of Done (DoD) and Acceptance Criteria	150
Identifying and Visualizing Risks	152
Tech Lead's Challenge with Cool Technologies	153
Summary	158
Potential Role Distributions	163
Reverse Mapping of Methods	173

The Team Dynamics and Contributing
Methods Map   174

The Five Dysfunctions and Opposing
Methods Map   178

Closing Words   182

References   184

Figures   188

FOREWORD

Over the years, countless conversations about software delivery with clients, with colleagues at Thoughtworks, with fellow technologists at conferences and industry events, solidified one belief for me: software development is now more than ever a team sport. Having the best technology, even the best technologists, isn't as important as having the team members collaborate effectively.

Teams should have a large degree of autonomy, they should rely on self-organization and continuous improvement where possible, and across the team competence in the technology stack is a must. In my experience, though, most high performing software delivery teams also have someone in a leadership role who is both a strong technologist and a good leader. This is not to say that project managers and coaches aren't important – they are – but a tech lead is often the person who is crucial in getting the team into the zone of high performance and to keeping them there.

In this book, Mesut, who I count myself fortunate to have as a colleague and a technology leader at Thoughtworks, draws on his experience and shines a light on the fundamental pillars of effective technical leadership. It starts with the human aspects of leading a team – creating psychological safety, the state in which team members feel they can be authentic and make themselves vulnerable. This concept was reinforced by Google's research project Aristotle which identified psychological safety as the number one predictor of high performing teams.

Drawing on this influential research, on the book Five Dysfunctions of a Team by Patrick Lencioni, and the DORA Metrics Mesut constructs a clear framework. This framework becomes the mental map you'll use to navigate the diverse practices introduced in the discussion of the three pillars: leadership, technical excellence, and value.

This book is a comprehensive collection of practical guidance for anyone embarking on the exciting and challenging journey of technical leadership. It's a journey of growth, not just for your team, but for yourself as well. As you delve deeper into its pages, remember − the most powerful tools you possess are your own authenticity, humility, and a genuine desire to empower those around you.

Embrace the journey, and let this book be your compass!

Erik Doernenburg

Acknowledgements

I am grateful to Erik Doernenburg for his foreword and count myself very lucky to have his words for the book.

I would like to sincerely thank Kapil Dube, Felix Holzäpfel-Stein, Andreas Klumpp, Sarah Schmid, Cengizhan Bayrak for their invaluable feedback on the work and Eveline Söder for her proofreading. My gratitude goes to Heidi Gehring not only for her feedback, but also for her motivating me to start writing about technical leadership.

I have to express my gratitude to all my colleagues from all around the world I have worked with since I started my career. Without the experience I had with them, I could not imagine that this hard work would come out.

Thousand thanks to my family and friends, who have been supporting me non-stop all the time. Thank you for being there!

About The Author

Mesut Ayata is a technology leader with almost two decades of experience. He is passionate about creating high performance teams, technical excellence, building safe environments, effective technical leadership, mentoring and enabling people. He is currently working as Principal Developer at Thoughtworks and so far served in different roles in organizations while leading multiple cross functional teams and technical leads. He has many years of solid hands-on experience in Mobility, Automotive, Digital Transformation areas with a wide range of technology stack from on-prem to cloud solutions, architecture and modern development practices.

He completed Oxford University - Executive Leadership Programme from Said Business School in 2022, holding a Masters degree (2010) from the

Informatics Institute and a Bachelor degree (2007) from Electrical & Electronics Engineering at METU. Mesut's hobbies can be listed as listening to music, playing musical instruments, woodwork, biking, hiking, traveling, dancing, photography and going into nature.

If you want to connect, send your ideas or give him feedback, you are more than welcome.
Links below.

Audience

This book is particularly for Tech Leads in their early career or people who would like to become a Tech Lead such as Senior Developers, Senior Software Engineers, Software Engineers or Software Developers. Moreover, it could be a good fit for people with other roles that would like to switch to technical leadership, such as Data Engineers, Data Scientists and Architects as well. Product owners, who are working with Tech Leads, could also benefit from the book through understanding the development practices, communication with Tech Leads, team dynamics, team performance, value focus and more.

Lastly, I hope and believe that anybody who is interested in creating high performance teams and running a Software Development Team effectively can benefit from the book.

I try my best to give methods, tips and guidelines for Effective technical leadership. I will mostly focus on reflections from my experience, so that it is more realistic and solid.

Introduction

Several years ago when I was asked to serve the Tech Lead role in a small team, I was pretty excited and happy to accept the challenge. Back then I was already serving in different software engineering roles in various environments, projects and platforms for more than 10 years, I had solid experience in the tech stack we used and I was pretty comfortable with the tools and the architecture. My heavy contribution to development was not only recognized by my team members, but also by my stakeholders outside my team. This made me feel confident about the new role. And that is how I started my journey on technical leadership.

It was my new role, and I had a strong motivation to be successful. It did not take long for me to realize that my coding skills and expertise in the technologies were still fundamental, but alone not enough to lead a development team. It was not clear what success meant for me.

What is success though, is it:

- Creating a safe environment?
- Making sure that delivery is on time?
- Building trust inside and outside the team?

- A good stakeholder management? Finding meaning and purpose in what we are doing?
- A healthy team?
- or rather to create perfect software solutions?
- Driving an evolutionary architecture?
- An extensible codebase that is easy to onboard new developers?
- To use the latest best technologies?
- Applying best development practices, what are they?
- Growing people around me?
- Enabling, empowering and delegation?
- Building a high performance team?
- Making the team effective?
- ....
- Or all above? But in which priority order?

Of course I was not the first one having these questions or getting into such a challenge. Plus, there were people supporting me on my new challenge, there was guidance. However, I missed back then a comprehensive guide where many aspects come together, contained in one place.

I am writing this book to provide you with the content I missed back then. I hope this will be helpful on your journey and it will also cover and answer the questions above.

Effective Teams

To understand what effective teams mean, let's first make it clear what effective means. According to the Oxford Learners Dictionary:

"Effective (Adj.): producing the result that is wanted or intended; producing a successful result". [25]

We can then continue with the definition: *"Effective teams are teams which produce the intended result."* The intended result should be serving the values of the organization and should be inline with the strategy and goals. It should bring value to the organization. As it is reaching goals, it should be high performing as well. When we combine all these together, we can conclude:

"Effective teams are high performance teams that successfully generate the intended value".

Indeed, what is necessary to make the team effective? There is already comprehensive research about the dynamics of an effective team. A research at Google states five dynamics of an effective team: *[26]*

---

[25]https://www.oxfordlearnersdictionaries.com/definition/american_english/effective

[26]https://www.thinkwithgoogle.com/intl/en-emea/consumer-insights/consumer-trends/five-dynamics-effective-team/

- Psychological safety
- Dependability
- Structure and clarity
- Meaning
- Impact

To elaborate each of them a bit more in the order of importance (most important first):

1. Psychological safety	Feeling safe to take risks, admitting mistakes and not being afraid of failures. People can speak up when they need to
2. Dependability	Team members can rely on and help each other and complete tasks on time
3. Structure and clarity	Team members are clear on the expectations from themselves as well as the team goals
4. Meaning	People find a meaning for what they are doing, which helps them to contribute and become motivated
5. Impact	This is where the team members feel that their effort is transformed into a

	change in what the organization needs and aligned with their goals

As it can be inferred from the description above, it is stated in the research that:

"Who is on a team matters much less than how team members interact, structure their work, and view their contributions." [26]

This is an extremely interesting outcome, which somehow emphasizes the ways of working in a team, and that it should be more important than the skills of each individual.

[26]https://www.thinkwithgoogle.com/intl/en-emea/consumer-insights/consumer-tr ends/five-dynamics-effective-team/

Not surprisingly, another research done by Lencioni is also bringing results similar to five dynamics of an effective team. According to Lencioni, the five dysfunctions of a team [5] can be listed as:

- Absence of trust
- Fear of conflict
- Lack of commitment
- Avoidance of accountability
- Inattention to results

To elaborate each of them a bit more in the order of sequential impact (the initial reason first):

[5] The Five Dysfunctions of a Team by Lencioni

1. Absence of trust	This is the starting factor for low performance teams. In such teams, people are not feeling safe about asking for help and there are doubts about the intentions of people.
2. Fear of conflict	Absence of trust leads to fear of conflict, where people avoid jumping into important topics because they are afraid to take any personal risk
3. Lack of commitment	The conflict avoidance leads to lack of commitment, because nobody makes a decision and teams struggle to move forward
4. Avoidance of accountability	Another aspect here is accountability, as nobody wants to take a risk because they are afraid
5. Inattention to results	Finally, people don't pay attention to team results, because there is a lack of common focus and objectives. Instead, people are focusing on themselves.

When we look at the five team dynamics of an effective team and five dysfunctions of a team, we can clearly see how common they are, especially in emphasizing the safe environments.

Based on these studies and my experience, I can clearly see that trust and a safe environment are the most important aspects of an effective team. A question on how to get there might then naturally arise right now. This is what we are going to cover in this book, especially with methods in the three pillars section.

So far, we have discussed the aspects of effective teams, and let's also check whether there are some signals understanding how a team is performing.

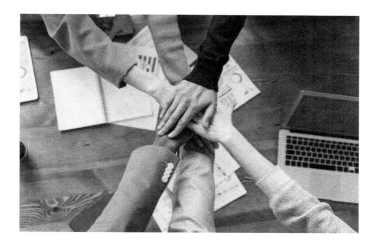

High Performance Team

According to research done by the DORA [2] team, the performance of a team is tightly connected to some measurable metrics. DORA metrics [2] , in other words four key metrics, are one of the famous approaches to understand how a team is performing. Basically, there are four metrics that are taken into the account to understand how well an organization is performing.

- **Deployment frequency**: How often an organization successfully releases to production

- **Lead time for changes**: The amount of time it takes a commit to get into production

- **Change failure rate**: The percentage of deployments causing a failure in production

- **Time to restore service**: How long it takes an organization to recover from a failure in production

As you can see, the higher the deployment rate is, the higher the performance is. The shorter the time for restoration, the better it is. The high adaptability for change is measured by lead time for changes.

---

[2]https://cloud.google.com/blog/products/devops-sre/using-the-four-keys-to-mea
sure-your-devops-performance

These metrics are indeed well aligned with agile principles and continuous integration and continuous delivery. Based on its nature, it promotes agile approach, incremental improvements and small deployments, and quick recoveries. I will explain how.

- You need to deploy often to increase the deployment frequency which is in line with continuous delivery, which states that the software is always in a releasable state [16]
- To decrease the lead time, you better deploy smaller changes, and create incremental user stories which are fitting to the incremental development
- As you deploy a lot, you may still have failures, but the failure rate is potentially low because you deploy often
- Besides, small changes are easy to follow and fix, or even revert back when necessary which is good for the time to restore metric

There are tools automating the tracking of these four key metrics, so short search could bring you some solutions already. Indeed, even once in a while checking these results could give you an overview. I believe that this in general helps the team think in an agile way with certain observations

---

[16]https://martinfowler.com/bliki/ContinuousDelivery.html

thanks to these metrics instead of a subjective approach. And that should be the goal, keeping the mindset agile. You want to have an idea about how your team is performing?

Take the DORA quick check [27]

Based on these researches and agile principles; my interpretation of a high performance team is actually pretty close to what I understand from an agile team:

- People supporting each other
- High level of interaction within the team
- Customer focused and value oriented
- Time to market is short
- Autonomous and capable of building the intended product(s) on its own
- Can adapt to changes fast
- Can identify and fix bugs fast

A high performance team delivers fast, makes the necessary changes and enhancements in the product(s) fast. The development and products can fail often, but recovers quickly. Although the definition seems to be relatively simple, how to achieve that is not so straightforward.

---

[27]https://dora.dev/quickcheck/

Leadership

Effective Technical Leadership

We now have an understanding for an effective team and how to measure that. We base it on certain researches such as dynamics of an effective team [26], dysfunctions of a team [5] and four key metrics (DORA metrics) [2] in the previous section.

That means, effective technical leadership is creating an effective team and leading for success. This includes several aspects, such as creating a safe environment, building trust, establishing feedback culture, increasing collaboration inside the team, ensuring knowledge distribution, finding a meaning at work, driving an evolutionary architecture, applying modern development practices, establishing a value based thinking and many more.

In my opinion, there are methods to achieve these and I will share them with you through the book.

---

[2]https://cloud.google.com/blog/products/devops-sre/using-the-four-keys-to-measure-your-devops-performance
[5]The Five Dysfunctions of a Team by Lencioni
[26]https://www.thinkwithgoogle.com/intl/en-emea/consumer-insights/consumer-trends/five-dynamics-effective-team/

Besides, we assume that there is a Tech Lead in a team, who covers all these methods, ways and responsibilities. Potential different setups are included in the Potential Role Distributions section in the end.

The Three Pillars

Effective teams require effective technical leadership. Remember that the five dynamics of an effective team are psychological safety, dependability, structure and clarity, meaning and impact. [26] Similarly the dysfunctions of a team are absence of trust, fear of conflict, lack of commitment, avoidance in accountability and inattention to results. [5]

There are many definitions about leadership. In my opinion, **leadership** is the ability to influence people, motivate them towards achieving a common goal, supporting and growing them as well. In the context of an effective team, leaders can have a lot of influence and they are responsible for many dynamics of effective teams. Especially providing a safe environment and building trust, giving structure and clarity, motivating people for higher commitment and growing people so that everybody can contribute and rely on each other are the main aspects of **leadership**.

[5]The Five Dysfunctions of a Team by Lencioni
[26]https://www.thinkwithgoogle.com/intl/en-emea/consumer-insights/consumer-trends/five-dynamics-effective-team/

According to agile principles [1], continuous attention to **technical excellence** and good design enhances agility. When we also take the DORA metrics [2] into account, we see how important it becomes to have frequent releases and faster recovery times. These are indeed easier to achieve as the team gets closer to continuous integration and continuous delivery. In this approach there is an automation in delivery and this eliminates the delays and waiting times, enables the team to deliver more often and recover from failures sometimes even in minutes. (We will touch on this topic in one of the three pillars in detail.)

Martin Fowler relates **technical excellence** tightly with continuous integration and continuous delivery [4], as this shows that the team is at a maturity level that is high performing. Remember that, frequent delivery is also in line with agile principles and enables the team to adapt to change faster, as it is delivering more often and incrementally. Faster recovery times are also good for customer satisfaction, where customer focus is at the center of agile principles.

[1]https://agilemanifesto.org/principles.html
[2]https://cloud.google.com/blog/products/devops-sre/using-the-four-keys-to-measure-your-devops-performance
[4]https://www.youtube.com/watch?v=Avs70dZ3Vlk

20

Considering the impact dynamic of an effective team, together with inattention to results of dysfunctions of a team, we can understand how the **value** a team brings is an important aspect of an effective team. Besides, according to agile principles [1], customer satisfaction, bringing customer **value** as well as valuable software are pretty important. In the definition of effectiveness, we have also stated that effectiveness is tightly related to generating wanted, intended results, producing a successful result.

All these are stating the essence of the **value** generated by the team.

When we combine all these aspects, I strongly believe and have experienced that, effective technical leadership stands on three pillars: leadership, technical excellence and value. To make it more clear, below is a picture:

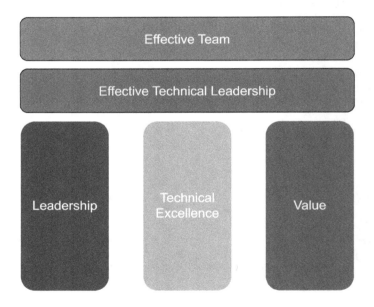

Figure 1: The Three Pillars of Effective Technical Leadership

Effective teams require effective technical leadership. Effective technical leadership stands on three pillars.

The leadership pillar is about creating a safe environment, building trust within the team and bringing structure, clarity and direction to team members. Leadership includes being an influencing leader of the team, a mentor, a guide and serving the team members and the organization.

The technical excellence pillar focuses on software engineering methods and principles, development and delivery practices such as continuous integration and continuous delivery in order to achieve a high performance team.

The value pillar is to ensure that the team is delivering high value aligned with the strategic goals of the organization. Here, the Tech Lead ensures that each technological solution is either solving or helping to solve a business problem, so that it is bringing value.

Tech Lead's ultimate goal is to create an effective team and lead for success. In my opinion, it is a challenging task and you need to master these three pillars in order to achieve this goal.

Notes

How to read tables?

Within many methods in the next sections, you will see a small table in the beginning showing what that particular method solves or serves for. This could be helpful for you to pick up certain tasks / methods to apply based on your team needs.

To illustrate:

Topic: Tech Huddles

Goal	Increasing collaboration
	Evolutionary architecture
	Teamwide decisions
Supports team dynamic(s)	Dependability
Opposes team dysfunction(s)	Absence of trust
	Fear of conflict
	Lack of commitment

In this table, tech huddle's goals are increasing collaboration, helping for evolutionary architecture and having teamwide decision making. It supports the dependability dynamic of an effective team while decreasing absence of trust, fear of conflict and lack of commitment. When Tech Lead applies this method, namely tech huddles, they are already putting a step ahead for an effective team with the above explanation.

The **symbol:** You may encounter this symbol, this is set for highlighting tip(s) for the relevant topic.

The **symbol:** You may also encounter this symbol, this is set for giving scenario(s) for the relevant topic.

Leadership

First Pillar: Leadership

I strongly believe that leadership is the ability to influence people, motivate them towards achieving a common goal, supporting and growing them as well. It is about building trust, creating a safe environment in a team and making the team members rely on each other. It is listening, giving directions, structure and clarity, serving and helping people on their journey and growth, empowering, enabling and delegation. All these are tightly connected to the dynamics of an effective team as we already mentioned in the previous section.

Building Trust: 5 Golden Rules

According to Lencioni, absence of trust in a team is the most prominent dysfunction of a team. [5] I have also experienced that building trust is one of the most important aspects of a leader. As a Tech Lead, you need to lead by example and try your best to build trust between you and your team members. Because you need to motivate them towards a common goal, that requires trust in between.

In this section, I will mention ways to build trust between you and your team members.

Rule 1: Listen

Goal	Building trust
Supports team dynamic(s)	Psychological safety
Opposes team dysfunction(s)	Absence of trust

More than a decade ago at work, I was unhappy about a situation. I asked my Tech Lead back then to talk about it and we had a meeting. He carefully listened to me and he started the conversation by, "I see your point, and I can imagine that it is a difficult situation." He asked open questions to understand it better before suggesting any solution. He was not sure if he could help me with that. However, regardless of the outcome, I was already feeling better after talking with him. It felt safe that I opened up, no regret. I trusted him more. This was leading by example, and it was a good learning for me how I can handle these conversations in the future.

I have also experienced different cases, where I felt I was not heard. Of course this can depend on several factors, everybody has their own life and we may not react to things the way we would always like to. Still, in my opinion, even if we can not solve people's problems, we should try our best to listen to them.

People feeling heard is an essential part of building trust. Try to provide them what they need. Even if you can not give it, hearing them and listening to their points of view will help to build trust. This is also one aspect of empathy.

I have experienced so many times that listening is an unbeatable powerful tool. Many times more than speaking. For instance; Does somebody have a complaint?. No matter if I agree or disagree. I have seen so often, when I just wait and let them speak, it is establishing a better environment to start with.

Do you want to say something without interrupting the other person? One way to make sure that your counter partner finishes their point is just to wait for around 5 secs after their last word. This will provide a safe space for the person to speak up and a feeling of being heard.

Is the person keeping silent? Ask open ended questions, and show your interest by asking questions about their points. Do not judge and simply listen actively.[9]

---

[9]https://www.ccl.org/articles/leading-effectively-articles/coaching-others-use-active-listening-skills/

Rule 2: Involve in Decision Making

Goal	Motivation
	Ownership
	Building trust
	Team spirit
Supports team dynamic(s)	Impact
	Meaning
Opposes team dysfunction(s)	Lack of commitment
	Inattention to results

This is one of the most powerful approaches in gaining trust and motivating people. Your team members will build respect for you, and eventually trust when you involve them in decision making, they will count on you; since you count on them. Simply include them in decision making, for instance in architectural discussions, ask their opinion. You agree or disagree, that is a separate story, but make sure that their point is evaluated or represented. When you disagree, try to state your thoughts with some facts instead of personal preferences.This will lead by example and motivate other members to also state their thoughts with facts and objectives.

When people feel that their ideas and suggestions are evaluated at work, they will have a feeling of ownership, which will increase the intrinsic motivation, following an increase in commitment and finally the impact of the team.

💡 When discussions are crucial, set a clear goal and limit the discussion duration. Sometimes, giving a break could help to move forward and even for finding a solution and coming to an agreement.

Rule 3: Do not Micromanage

Goal	Motivation
	Ownership
	Building trust
	Team spirit
Supports team dynamic(s)	Psychological safety
	Impact
Opposes team dysfunction(s)	Lack of commitment
	Inattention to results

Software development is a task that includes thinking to solve problems. This requires a certain level of focus. Micromanaging is for many developers something unacceptable. When you know that a team member is capable of driving a solution, give them the space. When not, get closer and support more.

Some developers are very much into working in their own ways. Let people do it their way as long as you don't have a strong counter argument based on some facts. You can understand it by asking the following questions:

- Is the driven solution following the tech guidelines?
- Is there any potential security leak?
- Any potential risk that creates unwanted situations?
- Is the progress of the development visible?

This is indeed something you need to approach per individual in the team. Some developers are more into their autonomy, some are more into calling for guidance. Help them when they need you and let them do it if they are doing it well. Again, what that well is, depends on the expectations, time constraints and other conditions the team is currently in.

Rule 4: No Finger Pointing

Goal	Building trust
	Team spirit
Supports team dynamic(s)	Psychological safety
Opposes team dysfunction(s)	Absence of trust

When something fails, carry it as a team and try to focus on solving it first. Afterwards, without finger-pointing anyone, try to find ways on how to avoid the problem in the future.

At this point it is crucial to apply prime directive [8] even if it is not a retrospective session.

---

[8]https://www.thoughtworks.com/en-de/insights/blog/applying-prime-directive-beyond-retrospective

This is what prime directive states:

"Regardless of what we discover, we understand and truly believe that everyone did the best job they could, given what they knew at the time, their skills and abilities, the resources available, and the situation at hand."

💡 Talk about the problem itself instead of who caused that.

For instance, do NOT say: "X has pushed the code and the prod failed."

Instead say: "According to the alarms we get, we have encountered a problem in production, the widget seems failing to load. Shall we look at that?"

Goal	Building trust
	Bringing clarity
Supports team dynamic(s)	Psychological safety
	Structure and clarity
	Meaning
Opposes team dysfunction(s)	Absence of trust

Most of the team members are focusing on their particular task while the Tech Lead keeps an eye on the big picture as well as understanding the upcoming tasks and challenges. Tech Leads are responsible to inform their teams early enough for these points. This may sound a distracting approach, but actually motivating because the team members will have a clear understanding of the upcoming topics.

Another important case for communication is when Tech Lead needs to drive for something else than what the team is expecting. In this case, it is pretty important to take time, explain and try to bring facts why it has to be done so. I know this is challenging, but trust me, it is more important how you approach it than what it actually is.

Creating a Safe Environment

Goal	Building trust
	Foster innovation
	Motivation
Supports team dynamic(s)	Psychological safety
Opposes team dysfunction(s)	Absence of trust
	Fear of conflict

As a leader, it is a big part of your responsibility to provide an environment where people trust each other, feel safe, clear on expectations and goals and work in high engagement. These aspects play a critical role in high performance teams. [26] [5]

Your role has a big responsibility: To create a safe environment. This has two main aspects.

[5] The Five Dysfunctions of a Team by Lencioni
[26]https://www.thinkwithgoogle.com/intl/en-emea/consumer-insights/consumer-trends/five-dynamics-effective-team/

One is about the atmosphere in the team, such as people feeling safe about expressing their opinions, being heard and growing all together. This is about building trust, communication, getting to know each other well, sharing knowledge, avoiding silos, feedback culture, core values, clear expectations and many more.

The other is that the development is safe, that when people make mistakes such as introducing bugs, the impact is likely to be small and recovery from failure is fast. This way, people will be encouraged to be innovative and effective, because they know that the impact of failure is small. This is related to continuous delivery and how to get there.

It is the Tech Lead's main responsibility to provide this environment to people with the above aspects. Only then people can be enabled and empowered to grow and deliver effectively.

Goal	Knowledge distribution
	Building trust
	Growing people
	Team spirit
Supports team dynamic(s)	Dependability
Opposes team dysfunction(s)	Absence of trust

Once you are progressing in creating a safe environment, which is the base for high performance teams, you can now focus on growing people around you. Remember that, growing people is a typical skill of leaders. Learning by doing is a great tool, we all know that engineers love it. Therefore, delegation becomes critical for growing people.

However, delegation should come with enabling and empowering. Because, without necessary skills and tools, your teammates may fail big and this can harm their motivation to learn and innovate.

Enabling is to help people grow in the relevant skills in order to deliver certain tasks. This is learning. Sometimes this happens through direct knowledge distribution sessions such as tech huddles. Assume that the team's applications are running on AWS Kubernetes and the team is having a "You build, you run" approach. In this setup understanding how Kubernetes, EKS etc work in AWS and running certain actions when necessary could be a good enabling case.

Another way is simply working together such as pair programming etc. As Tech Lead, you create an environment where people share knowledge. However, this is not limited to your team members, but also covers you. Despite your limited time, it is essential to spend time with your developers for coding together in between. Tech Lead has solid experience in the tech stack and should share this knowledge by also pair programming together with especially inexperienced developers. We will cover the pair programming topic in the next sections.

Empowering is indeed, providing the necessary tools so that people can execute their tasks. This is for instance, access to certain environments, working with a friendly IDE, having a running hardware etc.

Once you have these working well, it will be safer to delegate, because they will know what they are doing better. In fact, this will still not prevent people from making mistakes. Forcing no mistakes should not be an approach of an effective leader either, but how to make the impact to a minimum is the question. Here comes the technical excellence and best development practices, so that the team mitigates the impact of a human mistake, bug or any error to a minimum. We will talk about this also in the next sections.

Goal	Motivating team members
Supports team dynamic(s)	Dependability Impact
Opposes team dysfunction(s)	Absence of trust

One other aspect of great leaders is their humility in the team. They actively try to make their team members' work visible by getting out of the spotlight and letting them shine. This also includes motivating and supporting them to experience inter team communication, as well as contacting stakeholders. These skills are part of leadership, that any developer needs to grow into if they are interested in leadership. As a Tech Lead, part of your role is to help your team members grow in these skills as well.

Here it is vital that the Tech Lead provides the necessary support during this challenge. This is also part of delegation work that the Tech Lead handles.

Goal	Unlocking inefficiency
	Generating results
	Building trust
	Ensuring team mindset
Supports team dynamic(s)	Psychological safety
	Impact
Opposes team dysfunction(s)	Fear of conflict

It is not unusual that people have different opinions and they dive into deep discussions. To a certain extent it is useful and necessary for a team to be innovative. However, sometimes it can get pretty complicated, overwhelming and counter productive. There could also be an incident in production and an immediate action is necessary, where stress level could be high. These lead to some challenging discussions. Here are some examples of these cases:

- **Non-ending discussions**: It is nice to discuss technical topics, but sometimes i.e. in tech huddles, it can also be overwhelming if the team can not come to a conclusion. Topics can lead into other topics and they may lose the track of the actual topic and goal of the discussion. This is not efficient when it comes to time management. No conclusion, no outcome or progress means actually a waste of time.

- **Over engineering / solve far future problems**: Developers may also tend to do over engineering and solve far future problems assuming that they will occur one day. As the discussion continues, the assumption may be perceived as a fact which forces them to solve it as soon as possible.

- **Winning a discussion**: Especially in unsafe environments, people tend to try winning arguments rather than finding the best for the team and the end user. The discussion can be stuck between a group of people inside a big group. People try to invalidate the arguments of others instead of being constructive and focusing on the solution.

- **Defensive mode turned on**: During discussions in unsafe environments improvement suggestions may be perceived offensive which can make some members defensive. Once this mode is there, it is not easy to get people back to a constructive position again.

It is the Tech Lead's responsibility to identify these moments and find a way to bring the team back to a constructive state.

Above are listed only some and there can be more challenges. You need to monitor the ambiance and react when you feel such a bottleneck. It is not easy to solve them, but there are some methods to try:

- **Call for focus**: Sometimes it is good to remind developers the phrase "out of scope", try to stick to the topic under discussion. Saying *"I see your point, but it is a different topic. Let's please focus on the problem."* may be helpful.

- **Remind value based thinking**: Asking below questions can help:
    - What kind of value is this bringing to development, delivery and user?
    - What are we solving here?

- **Avoid ping-pong discussions**: This is a moment, where the discussion is stuck between two attendees in a big group. This is not the most efficient way of consuming the time. Asking this can help: What do others think, any ideas?

- **Empathy:** Before suggesting improvements about some software piece or a system, start first by asking questions to understand the reasoning behind. This will pull the relevant people into discussion, they will have a chance to explain themselves and have a feeling of being heard. Besides, there may be things that are yet not known or not visible to you. Keep prime directive [8] in mind.

Sometimes, these ways are also not sufficient. You can then timebox the discussion and stop at some point. Afterwards, maybe have a 1on1 with the individuals and try to understand them a bit better, and drive your approach from there.

---

[8]https://www.thoughtworks.com/en-de/insights/blog/applying-prime-directive-beyond-retrospective

Goal	Building trust
	Being approachable
	Growing people
Supports team dynamic(s)	Psychological safety
	Dependability
Opposes team dysfunction(s)	Absence of trust

This is to make sure that you separate time for your team members when necessary. It can be regular or on demand. 1on1s do not have a particular format, it is dependent on you and your team member how to shape it. I do often use it to:

- Create or improve my connection
- Give a space for team member and listen
- Asking open ended questions to understand how they are doing
- Asking how I can support them
- Informing them about actions taken (if any) previously

Indeed, having a more clear structure can be really helpful for more effective interaction. Consider keeping track of the highlights of your talk, take actions if necessary and then follow up in the next round. Your team members would feel better when you come up with some results of their points/questions etc afterwards and this will help build trust.

1on1s are also a great time for mentoring and growth talks. Consider asking the following questions:

- What are your team member's goals?
- How can you support them on their journey?
- What are the pain points and how can you help them to solve it?
- ...

💡 Make sure you keep track of the topics, actions and progress per team member. Otherwise it could get very complex pretty soon and you may start to forget the actions, topics etc. Remember that, for you this could be one of the many topics you have on your table, but for your teammate it could be a very high priority.

💡 As Tech Lead, you need to watch your time and how you spend it. Making regular 1on1s with all team members could very easily drain your time and fill up your calendar. You can start with regular meetings, but try to reach a state where on demand is enough. Set the frequency based on the needs of the team member.

Goal	Building trust
	Growing all together
Supports team dynamic(s)	Psychological safety
Opposes team dysfunction(s)	Absence of trust
	Fear of conflict

An essential aspect of a safe environment and growing as a leader is your approach to feedback. Feedback is crucial to understand and reflect how your actions and work are perceived on people's side. It is indeed, a culture often takes time to set. There are two aspects of feedback: Giving and receiving.

While giving feedback, pay attention to the below points:

- Set your communication from your point of view. What you tell is your perception, share it clearly with some information. Share data and facts if available. Do not judge and do not include any judging statement. Be open and keep the door open. Avoid very sharp statements
- Be constructive, set your perspective to share things to improve, not that people are wrong

As an example:

"Yesterday in X meeting, if I remember right, I heard from you that … I was a bit confused. I felt that … I believe that we could do it this way … What do you think"

While receiving feedback, first of all, be happy that people are honest with you and sharing their perspective. It takes time and courage for people to come and give you feedback. They don't have to. Be aware of how valuable it is, appreciate their effort. Secondly, pay attention to the points below.

- Make sure, you don't interrupt and listen to the end
- First reaction: Thank them for the feedback and express your gratitude
- Be curious, ask questions in order to understand people's perspective instead of judgment
- Do not defend!

Keep in mind that, when people share their feedback, it is their perspective, perception and reality. It does not have to fit what you do or think. You don't have to agree with the arguments, but in the end it is the other person's reality. Ask questions and try to understand what you can learn from that.

How to set the feedback culture? Yes, it starts with you as a role model. Plus, there are also some events that you can bring to the team, which will improve the overall feedback culture. Below we talk about some of them.

Feedback Forms

You can send feedback forms with some open ended questions to get a glimpse of how people perceive your actions. In general, your questions can be around three points below, if you don't have any particular topic.

- What do I do well?
- What can I improve?
- Any recommendations?

The forms with anonymous answering options help people to react more transparently to your questions.

Speedback

It is a teamwide feedback activity, where team members talk to each other as 1on1 very shortly for giving and receiving feedback, i.e. two minutes each. [10]

Then members rotate, and in the end all the team members meet all the other team members. This will help all the members to connect and get a reflection from outside on how they are doing.

---

[10]https://www.thoughtworks.com/en-de/insights/blog/what-speedback-and-how-run-it-using-zoom-breakout-rooms

Goal	Building trust
Supports team dynamic(s)	Psychological safety
Opposes team dysfunction(s)	Absence of trust Fear of conflict

It would be very nice when there is a strong feedback culture, but in reality, it is not mature in many organizations and people may feel uncomfortable with giving or receiving feedback. This could unfortunately be the case no matter how you try to be open and welcoming. On top of the company dynamics, there could also be some challenges based on your role. Being in a leadership position like Tech Lead may put team members in an uncomfortable state because of the power dynamics. Another may be that there is not enough trust yet, especially if you are new in the role. So, these aspects do not make the situation better.

Another aspect is about your perception of a certain case, which does not necessarily be the same as others. There is a cultural aspect of communication, where for the same fact people tend to react differently not only based on their individual preferences, but also with some influence of their culture. Erin Meyer [28] investigates this topic in depth how culture is influencing our reactions and communication. Although you can not know all the cultures and how people would react in certain cases, still being aware of the existence of differences helps to understand and read the situations better.

However, as a leader, you still need to understand how you are doing and get some reflection from the team. Are people giving you constructive feedback? If not, please do not think that you are doing everything perfectly, it is more likely that people may not be feeling comfortable around you to tell what is not going well.

[28] https://erinmeyer.com/books/the-culture-map/

You suggest an improvement idea and people did not comment on that, no questions or improvement suggestions are made. It is unlikely that people have no idea on your suggestion. This could indeed mean that some people may feel uncomfortable around you to comment on your ideas.

Sometimes people talk indirectly by asking questions instead of sharing their perspectives. This is indeed something that could be powerful in influencing. However, sometimes it could be hard to understand what the actual point is. In the end, what people are talking about, including their questions, somehow also reflect part of what they are thinking. Listen and think what they are talking about. Ask open ended questions to try to understand them better.

Goal	High performing team members
Supports team dynamic(s)	Psychological safety Dependability Impact
Opposes team dysfunction(s)	Absence of trust Fear of conflict Lack of commitment

It is the people delivering value and building the product. That is why it is crucial to know how they are doing. Therefore you need data! Say that you are well connected to individual team members and having regular 1on1s with all, but what about understanding the overall picture a bit better?

One way of achieving that is having regular or irregular health checks including all team members in between to understand the hidden problems, or make them more visible. Indeed, it may not make all the challenges visible, but can bring a high level overview of how people are doing and what they are struggling with. I recommend doing health checks anonymously, so that you can collect more honest answers. Team Health checks help you to have a snapshot on what people are thinking, how they are doing and what they want indeed.

There is no particular format on how to do it, nor a concrete period of time. If you have enough budget, you can even use 3rd party tools as well. Manual or automated, there are mainly three aspects of the process.

- Collection of the feedback
- Understanding, comparison and prioritization
- Taking actions
- Evaluation of outcomes

Based on my experience, I can say that it takes time to collect feedback, prioritize and take actions. Therefore, these checks are more meaningful to have a couple of times a year. I..e every 3 months etc.

On the other hand, in practice, even every retrospective meeting could also be used to have a form of team health check. However, having dedicated time could help. I recommend the following for more transparent and efficient health checks for retros.

- Make it anonymous
- Before the start of each session, do an anonymous safety check. It is important that everybody feels safe before the start of the retrospective. Everybody should feel safe and even if one member of the team feels unsafe, then change the retro to understand how you can establish safety again
- Make sure to cover three aspects of what makes them happy, what to improve and any ideas to share [30], [31]

Sharing the results with the team is as important as taking actions based on the input. You don't have to find the solutions on your own, but as a Tech Lead, it is expected that you lead to find actionable solutions when applicable together with the team.

[30]https://www.scrum.org/resources/what-is-a-sprint-retrospective
[31https://www.atlassian.com/team-playbook/plays/retrospective

Roles and Responsibilities

Goal	Clarifying expectations Increasing commitment
Supports team dynamic(s)	Structure and clarity
Opposes team dysfunction(s)	Lack of commitment Avoidance of accountability

Clear roles and responsibilities play a critical role in creating high performance teams. Missing clarity here could end up in chaos or fights in a team. We need clear roles and responsibilities for each team in order to make it perform high. So, what are roles and responsibilities and how to shape them? Try to understand the following:

- What are the tasks the team have to take care of on a daily, regular or non periodic basis?
- Which roles are responsible for which tasks and who is filling which role?
- How clear are the expectations set?

In a high performing agile team, developers, designers and product managers could work together to create the best user experience for their customer.

This is also inline with the agile principle [1] "Business people and developers must work together daily throughout the project."

How to find the exact definition of who has what responsibilities, is possible via the team, product and organization dynamics. For instance, the business people can be represented in a development team with different names such as Product Owner, Product Manager, Project Manager, Business Analyst etc. Sometimes, developers are called Software Engineers etc. So, these names depend on the circumstances but what we need to make sure of is to cover all the responsibilities that have to be handled in order to build the necessary products.

So, how do we find the roles and responsibilities then? Ok, why not decide on that together with the team through a workshop, called roles and responsibilities workshop?

---

[1]https://agilemanifesto.org/principles.html

In such an exercise, ideally all the team members, but at least all the representatives of the potential roles should be present. Basically, this can be done in order:

1. List all the responsibilities done or should be done in the team
2. List the potential roles to cover all the above
3. Assign the responsibilities to the roles
4. Assign individuals to the roles
5. Celebrate

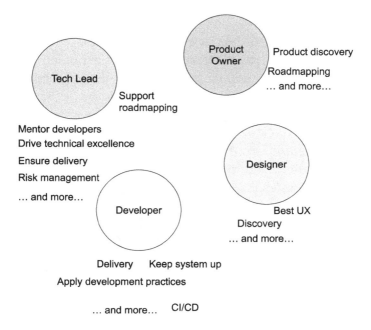

Figure 2: A draft roles and responsibilities workshop outcome

Just a very simple example above on how it would look like. Please take into consideration that role names, roles itself and the responsibilities around them are per team based, and it will vary.

Starting from the facts (i.e. the responsibilities that have to be done) and keeping the assignment of individuals to the end helps to create more professional and less emotional connection. Because, we talk about the roles and responsibilities, not the individuals.

This will not only help the team to check whether all the responsibilities are covered by the team, but also will bring clarity about what is expected from each role and indirectly from the individuals assigned to roles.

This exercise will also be helpful for you to understand what the team is expecting from you and what you can expect from your developers based on your and their responsibilities.

Expecting this exercise will solve every problem and bring 100% clarity on expectation management is not realistic though. However, my experience clearly shows that it will help in that direction by bringing some clarity.

Make sure that each team member has only one role!. Otherwise it could be not productive and even bring more harm than benefits, due to overload and confusion in responsibilities.

Goal	Increasing team spirit Aligning with organization values
Supports team dynamic(s)	Structure and clarity Meaning
Opposes team dysfunction(s)	Avoidance of accountability Inattention to results

Another very important aspect of a well functioning team is clearly defined core values. What are the core values of the team? Is it trust, transparency, technical excellence, continuous delivery and/or something else?

What about having a workshop and aligning them all together?

A core values and ways of working workshop could be particularly helpful here to address these needs. Basically the team discusses all together how they want to work and align on the values and ways of working as reference points to rely on.

I remember that this was once pretty challenging. I was a Tech Lead in a team of people with different working cultures. We did in the end, add continuous delivery to one of our core development methods. This was not easy and took many hours of discussions until we came to that point. But it was worth it.

In the end, the team aligns on many aspects of working together. For instance, is pair programming a default working model? Trunk based development is preferred? And many more…
It is good to make the values and ways of working transparent, so that there is a standard approach in the team and people can expect a certain level of integrity about working together. This could be helpful in increasing the effectiveness of delivery.

How to Run?

A simple search on google can help you to find certain templates. Overall, I believe that a sample workshop could include the following steps:

- Start with an ice breaker
- Every team member notes down their values i.e. trust, transparency, safe environment etc
- All these values are then combined, even merged if possible for simplicity

- The team selects some of them, i.e. 5 most important by voting

All these results are then saved and visited in between. It is a reference point to rely on, because values do not change that often despite the change around product or strategic changes of an organization.

A similar approach can also be applied to ways of working. Here though, the focus would be how to deliver value, and somehow to find out the default ways to deliver value. In this context, the team tries to align as for example on the following.

- How to ship value? Pull requests or trunk based development?
- How do they share knowledge? I.e. pair programming, knowledge sharing sessions, tech huddles?
- How do they ensure quality? Test coverage, integration testing, testing pyramid etc..
- …

This creates a unified environment and aligns the team members on working together smoother, expectations from team members can become clearer.

💡 I really recommend doing such a workshop when creating a team, so that the teams align on a common approach for how to work together. That said, it is also important to visit these in between and re-run the workshop, as the team and goals evolve. In my experience, this took around a year, sometimes more, depending on how fast especially the team, but also the project was changing.

💡 If you see that people start diverging from each other in the aligned ways of working, that is a signal to do the workshop again.

Onboarding / Offboarding

Goal	Increasing team spirit
	Increasing speed in delivery
Supports team dynamic(s)	Dependability
	Impact
Opposes team dysfunction(s)	Absence of trust
	Inattention to results

Onboarding

Source:
https://www.pexels.com/photo/black-and-white-photo-of-people-boarding-an-und
erground-train-15848202/

74

We are in constant change all the time. The product changes, the requirements change, so do the team members! The question is:

How fast can a new member start delivering value?

To create a high performing team, your goal includes to minimize the duration that a developer becomes fully committed. I have seen that these actions can be pretty helpful to have a fast onboarding experience.

- An onboarding buddy
- Having a check list of all the steps necessary to provide the environment (accounts, access etc.)
- As much automation as possible. I.e. script for creating a local development environment.

For the offboarding, you are responsible for making sure that:

- All the critical information and knowledge are transferred to the team
- Accounts are deactivated.
- Passwords/keys for some common tools are rotated. i.e. Gitlab CI/CD Users.

Knowledge Distribution

Goal	Avoiding silos
	Increasing collaboration
	Sustainable delivery
Supports team dynamic(s)	Dependability
Opposes team dysfunction(s)	Absence of trust

Knowledge distribution among the team is one of the most characteristic representatives of how the team performs. It is totally normal that each member of the team has their own skills and maybe even focus points. However, that does not mean that there won't be overlap. Indeed, there should be. Why so? Silos indeed could bring a lot of value, but teams can bring more value and it is scalable and sustainable. I have the following questions for consideration:

- What if the "very expert" becomes sick or goes for vacation?
- Maybe quit the job?
- Have you heard about the bus factor?

- Do you want to go too fast and crash at some point, or do you want to go fast and deliver sustainably?

It is therefore very important that the individuals share their knowledge and expertise with other members in the team, so that the work can continue if some members are not available.

Knowledge distribution is not only necessary for the sake of the project, but also for the team morale. This helps the members feel more confident and relaxed, as the work can still progress without them as a person. The team is responsible for the progress, not an individual. This brings a more distributed and balanced ownership of topics among the team, and contributes to a good and healthy team spirit. There are ways to ensure knowledge sharing.

You are not responsible for teaching everybody everything, but you are responsible for making sure that the knowledge is somehow distributed among the team members. There are methods for achieving that such as pair programming, tech huddles etc and we are going to cover them in the technical excellence pillar.

💡 Do team members always tend to do similar tasks they always do? Kindly ask actively for changing areas and work on different topics. Use pair programming as a learning and knowledge sharing tool.

Goal	Knowledge distribution
	Increasing collaboration
	Evolutionary architecture
	Teamwide decisions
	Ownership
Supports team dynamic(s)	Dependability
Opposes team dysfunction(s)	Absence of trust
	Fear of conflict
	Lack of commitment

Tech huddles are recurring events where developers come together and discuss any technical and architectural topics, share their knowledge and learn from each other.

And yes, tech huddles help teams in multiple dimensions. Let's check it out:

Keep your developers up-to-date

We are living in such an era that a technology or tool popular now may not be that valid anymore in just a couple of years. Things are evolving pretty fast and it is both an opportunity and yet a challenge to be on track. Tech huddles can be used as a platform for developers to follow new trends, tools and technologies help the developers and finally the product to stay up to date.

Increase team engagement & contribute to safe environment

Being a place where several developers freely speak their mind, suggest ideas, ask questions and comment, tech huddles increase overall team engagement. This contributes to a safe environment thanks to increased communication and collaboration.

Knowledge sharing

Another motivation for tech huddles is to promote knowledge distribution among developers. This enables more people in the team per topic, mitigating silos which in return means sustainable development.

Promote innovation

Having an explicit discussion platform can help developers to think of new things and evolve the system. When many developers talk to each other, there may be things coming up that none of them has thought of individually before. Sharing ideas interactively can result in new and better ones.

Set the feeling of ownership

We are living in an era, where developers would like to have more autonomy and decide on their own for bringing their best solutions for the relevant business requirements instead of being told how to do things. Tech huddles can be a platform for ensuring technical excellence, increasing quality, decision making all together and taking the architecture and product to the next level. This helps them to have more ownership of the product, because they are part of the decision chain. More ownership means more engagement and in the end a high performance team.

Challenge the current system and revisit the architecture

Yet another advantage could be the discussions to decrease tech debt and improve the architecture. Architecture is something that evolves, given that the team wants to do so. An evolving architecture is only possible by people pushing for that. Tech huddles can give them the opportunity to challenge the existing architecture and push for improvements.

Clear impediments for development

There are several technical challenges developers face. Sometimes, it can be very helpful to bring it to a wider audience and ask for alternative solutions. Ideally, impediments should not wait for a tech huddle, rather should be solved ASAP. Still, there may be some points that are hindering developers from being more productive; i.e. a non-stable pipeline. Tech huddles provide developers with a platform to solve such problems and improve.

How to Organize?

Of course these can vary based on team and product, but in general there are similar patterns. Simply listing the topics for discussion and taking action afterwards is one way. Doing it weekly / biweekly is pretty common, but can also be even daily, monthly or on demand, that really depends. One way of listing topics is like below:

Upcoming topics

	Topic	Who	Content	Duration
1	Cloudfront	Sarah	How we can benefit from Cloudfront in our multi continental applications	30 min
2				

Past topics

	Date	Topic	Who	Content	Action
1	14.12. 2023	Restassured	Anna	An integration testing tool…	ADR added Test in staging
2					

In summary, tech huddles help team members to bring ideas, engage with each other, understand impediments, share knowledge and experience, and create an open discussion environment where innovation is enabled. Despite its challenges, it provides some must haves for a high performance team.

💡 To give every team member an opportunity to learn how to facilitate and drive conversations, consider rotating the facilitator each time.

Keep track of your To-Do list

I have witnessed how this is so much helping. It is not that difficult to get lost in details and tasks you want to do. Some people keep a personal Kanban Board, some just a To-Do list. Eitherway make sure that you keep track of what you need to do.

 Take the break you need

Your workload can get pretty overwhelming in a short time. Take the breaks you need. Everybody has a limit and the question is more about being sustainable and continuous than high performing short but having a burnout.

 **Prioritize**

You can not do everything you want to do. Remember, you have a task list, please keep it prioritized. It can change indeed, the worklife is pretty dynamic. Make sure you have a WIP (Work in Progress) limit. Project rules also apply to your daily life.

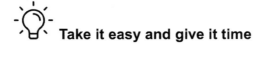 **Take it easy and give it time**

You want the team to be high performing, you set goals, follow best practices. This does not mean that it is gonna change until tomorrow. Keep in mind during your daily interactions to give people time, appreciate progress instead of expecting a big change to happen immediately.

Summary

In this section, I talked about leadership aspects, and provided some tips and methods to create an environment necessary for effective teams.

Creating a safe environment takes time. It includes establishing a feedback culture, building trust, listening, engaging, motivation, growing people, knowledge distribution, setting values, clear expectations and goals. Aligning on values could be helpful to have common perspectives.

It is crucial how to handle the critical moments or challenging situations. These are indeed an opportunity to grow as a team. To overcome these moments, trust and team values are essential. You play a critical role to drive these moments for a good outcome. I tried to explain this in driving challenging technical discussions.

As we are closing this section, now we are heading to the technical excellence pillar.

Technical
Excellence

Second Pillar: Technical Excellence

Many years ago when I was a fresh software engineer, I worked on projects where we tried to know every detail of a yet non existing product before we started any development. More than 100 pages of requirements document with another following of detailed description for the system architecture to be built were at the center of the process. This document even had function names with their parameters and how they call each other. Months of effort from many people put into each one before any start of development. I learned that each document should be as detailed as possible, so that we don't miss any point and can implement everything very smoothly and error free afterwards.

I was pretty convinced that we should know every detail to be built and every requirement of a product before we start any development. Once we have all the details, then we could start implementing for some year(s). Once we finish, the testing department will do the testing and they will check all the bugs and we fix them. Then we get the approval and we can release the product. Party time.

The intention was great and designed for perfection, yet, what this yielded often were delay in delivery, integration problems between partial product development of different departments, blockage, obstacles, unknowns, inflexibility for the new or changing requirements of the customer and unused but built functionality. This could have been differently though.

I don't think that we have solved all the problems above right now in the industry, but I do think that we have made some progress.

In this section, we are going to focus on technical excellence and some practices to reach that goal. This includes also some development practices and how to deliver value, i.e. continuous delivery.

It is actually a very debatable topic among developers and sometimes discussions can be challenging. Of course, these are not the only ways to achieve these steps. I wanted to provide this section, to give some preferences and guidance together with reasons behind. I have experienced that this way the teams are more effective, the products get into market sooner, the delivery is faster and less risky.

What is Technical Excellence?

I often experience that there is a big debate around here, especially on the definition. Many developers think that tech excellence is something to do with cool technologies. Some imagine it to be endless refactorings. Indeed, Martin Fowler brings clarity here. He relates technical excellence to continuous delivery. [4]

I really like this approach, since in order to reach a state like continuous delivery, the team should be very mature in the ways they develop software, the codebase, the quality, testability, maintainability and so on...

Not surprisingly, Google research [2] also connects many continuous delivery metrics such as deployment frequency, time to recover etc into critical metrics in defining how well the team is performing. We will come to this point also in the next pages.

[2]https://cloud.google.com/blog/products/devops-sre/using-the-four-keys-to-mea
sure-your-devops-performance
[4]https://www.youtube.com/watch?v=Avs70dZ3Vlk

In this section, I will focus on several development practices I have experienced so far, that help to achieve technical excellence and eventually high performance teams.

Pair Programming

Goal	Knowledge distribution
	Increasing collaboration
	High quality software
Supports team dynamic(s)	Dependability
	Impact
Opposes team dysfunction(s)	Fear of conflict

Pair Programming

Pair programming is an agile software development technique in which two programmers work together at one workstation. [14] Ensuring 4-eyes principle, namely two developers are developing code and actively looking at the same screen together, (even remotely using some tools) pair programming helps a lot for a higher quality of work. [13]

Pair programming not only ensures quality in the early stages of development, it is also one of the most important tools to avoid knowledge islands. It helps actively to distribute the knowledge among the team members. Yet another motivation, the pairs learn to work together and increase engagement.

On the other hand, pair programming can sometimes be too tiring. Besides, if the same pairs work all the time together, it can also lose its actual goal. The pairs can become so close to each other that they may feel like a sub-team inside the team. Moreover, knowledge is accumulated yet on kinda another island. But I have some good news, you can avoid that: Rotate pairs frequently and take breaks :)

Ideally in every sprint pairs can and should rotate. To make the rotation smooth and uninterrupted in development, it is good to have a pilot developer.

[13]https://www.techtarget.com/searchsoftwarequality/definition/Pair-programm.
[14]https://www.thoughtworks.com/en-de/insights/blog/seven-principles-pair-prog ramming-etiquette

In this setup, the pilot developer works on the respective ticket/task and the other pair is rotating. This ensures continuity of work while distributing the knowledge.

Let's also compare pair programming and pull requests a bit.

Pull requests (PRs) are of course also one way of ensuring quality. To put simply, a developer develops code on a branch for some time and when she finishes her code, she creates a pull request in order for her code to be reviewed. After the review finished, the code could be merged into the main branch and shipped. However, it has the following downsides:

- Waiting time for the review
- Ping-pong between the comments, fixes and yet another comment.
- Knowledge sharing may not be very effective through reviews

Pair programming is a different approach where there are no separate code reviews, rather two developers work and develop code together. Pair programming has the following advantages:

- No waiting time for code reviews, it is done during development
- Knowledge sharing is more effective while both pairs are part of development and they learn by doing

- Quality is ensured during development, not afterwards

While it has certain benefits, pair programming can also come with some challenges. It could be tiring and not everybody is confident about it, especially in the early stages. But these could be improved in time.

Following New Technologies

There have been and are going to be probably many more tools entering developer's daily life. It is beyond the scope of this book to cover these tools. However, it is expected from a Tech Lead to follow the trend, and not only to be open but also to drive the change in their team when applicable and bringing certain value.

Taking the Github Co-pilot as an example that recently entered our development life, it seems to be pretty beneficial in some cases. Here what you and your team members need to take into account is to use it effectively. Remember that, you will still need to review the code generated. So, the bigger code generation you ask, the longer time you need to review and prove that it works. [24]

I believe that it could be useful and it is not a replacement for pair programming, rather an extra tool which could increase the quality and delivery speed when used wisely. Tech Lead is there to balance between exploring new trends while bringing value as well as to make sure that the new technologies are used appropriately.

---

[24]https://www.thoughtworks.com/en-de/insights/blog/generative-ai/getting-started-with-github-copilot

Overall, the questions you should ask yourself is:

- How do you keep the track of new technologies?
- What are your learning opportunities?
- Which conferences should you and your team members join this year?
- Which learning platforms are you and your team following?

The answers to these questions depend on different factors, such as your project and/or career goals. But I believe that asking these questions and finding answers fitting to your needs are crucial.

Thoughtworks Technology Radar [36] is naturally designed for following new trends and learning from the experience of many people around the world. This could also be a source for learning about new tools and technologies you have not used before.

---

[36] https://www.thoughtworks.com/radar

Goal	Leveraging risks
	Automation
	High quality software
Supports team dynamic(s)	Dependability
	Impact
Opposes team dysfunction(s)	Inattention to results

Automated testing on the pipeline plays a critical role in continuous delivery. As a Tech Lead, you would like to deliver fast, and if an error occurs, you would like to catch it as soon as possible. Having a mature level of automated testing on the way to production not only makes things faster, but also safer. A mature level of automated testing is a must have capability to enable continuous delivery, so that it is safer to deploy continuously.

I have seen several times that some developers avoid writing even unit tests for small methods or classes. Reasoning behind is familiar: *"just one line of code"*, *"not necessary"*, *"time consuming"*, *"it is obvious"*, *"no business logic"*. I can imagine that some of the sentences are familiar to many of us.

Indeed, some code pieces may look very simple, but does that make it less important? I had once experienced how it was critical to have a simple test to mitigate human error as much as possible. Having an integration test (i.e. a WebMvcTest in spring framework) over a rest controller can give you faster feedback during development before even pushing your code. The test could be as simple as some lines of code.

I will list here some basic approaches to testing that you can keep in mind and use them based on your needs.

Test driven development (TDD) [6] is a way of development, where tests are not written separately after finishing the code, rather they are written first, make them fail and respective code is developed until the tests are green. This helps to ensure certain test coverage, understand the requirements from the developed feature better and challenge the development for a higher quality.

A typical TDD is so implemented:

- In order to write the test, developers should understand clearly what they expect from a method/function etc first
- Based on the signature of the method, now they can write a simple unit test
- The test will fail as the implementation is not done yet
- Code is not pushable until the test is green
- This enforces writing incrementally, because developers want to keep it soon green again
- Once it is green, commit
- Re-continue for the next test

---

[6]https://www.thoughtworks.com/insights/blog/test-driven-development-best-thin g-has-happened-software-design

In reality, TDD represents a high maturity level in testing.

What is the Right Level of Coverage?

There is also a lot of discussion about the test coverage. Some teams decide to have a minimum level, say 80% coverage goal to bring some sort of maturity in testing. I am personally not a fan of these settings. These levels can easily be cheated by no-value bringing tests just to cover more. In my opinion, tests are not the goal, rather ensuring high quality is the goal.

Mutation Testing

You can indeed measure the quality of tests by simply mutation testing. In mutation testing, the source code is changed and the tests are run afterwards. If then the tests fail, that means they are relevant. Here, it is aimed to see if some tests are failing after the source code is being changed. If no test is failing, it is an alarm! [35] There are even tools [34] doing them automated for you, though it is a bit slow compared to usual testing.

[34]https://pitest.org/
[35]https://www.techtarget.com/searchitoperations/definition/mutation-testing

Consumer Driven Contract Testing

Have you ever experienced that a change deployed in a team caused big problems in another team's service? If you are working in an environment where you have plenty of critical external dependencies, such as services, APIs etc, one way to mitigate the risk of wider system outages is to enable consumer driven contract (CDC) testing. [37], [38]

CDC's do need some effort in the beginning, but they are making the system safer by preventing integration problems that can occur after deployments of services inside and outside your team and domain.

💡 Overall, automated testing plays a critical role in continuous delivery. Different testing techniques and testing pyramid are important for you to grasp. You should have not only a good understanding of the testing pyramid, but also a good level of explanation and even convincing skills. Adding here more links for your reading. [39],[40]

---

[37]https://pactflow.io/what-is-consumer-driven-contract-testing/
[38]https://martinfowler.com/articles/consumerDrivenContracts.html
[39] https://martinfowler.com/articles/practical-test-pyramid.html
[40] https://martinfowler.com/testing/

Trunk Based Development

Goal	Faster and frequent delivery
	Automation
Supports team dynamic(s)	Impact
Opposes team dysfunction(s)	Inattention to results

Trunk based development is a way of delivering code on the main branch. Unlike the traditional way, features are not developed on branches and merged afterwards, rather all features are developed on the main branch and pushed directly without code review afterwards. Indeed, code review is done directly when developing for fast feedback, namely pair programming, and we have covered this topic in advance.

So, what does it make advantageous then?

Development on the feature branches can be seen as convenient, but it could have following downsides.

- The developers may not often update the feature branch, as this could lead to conflicts
- The code to integrate at a point to the main branch could get very big which can make the integration more complicated
- It could be hard to observe the impact of the merge into the main branch due to size of change

Trunk based development is on the other hand helping to solve these problems. All the developers develop on the main branch, every single change is reflected on other developments once the code is pushed or updated. Changes tend to be frequent but small by nature, which is easier to manage and serves the incremental development idea. [11]

[11]https://www.thoughtworks.com/en-de/insights/blog/enabling-trunk-based-deve
lopment-deployment-pipelines

As in the new setup, the features are also deployed during development, it is also likely that it is not ready to be presented to the end user. Feature toggles help here to experience the progress in another environment, i.e. staging, but keep the changes invisible to the end user by disabling it in the production environment. [12]

This way, it enables us to actually feel how the changes look like in another environment rather than production already. We have seen progress day by day and it helped us to mitigate the problems earlier.

Feature toggles are also enabling the Product Owners or other business stakeholders to have a feeling of a new feature in production before shipping it to the end users.

The internal stakeholders can test the new features and feel more confident or give feedback for improvements. Similarly it would also be used as a ground for A/B testing, where some features are shown to some portion of end users. Certain metrics and analytics can be applied on top and the behavior could be understood by how users react to new features, before it is rolled out to all customers.

---

[12]https://www.thoughtworks.com/en-de/insights/blog/managing-feature-toggles-teams

Goal	Highly available systems
	Customer satisfaction
Supports team dynamic(s)	Impact
Opposes team dysfunction(s)	Inattention to results

One of the key features of a high performance team is identifying and fixing the bugs fast. You have a well tested code and things are fine during development. However, things can still fail afterwards. It is not only the code, but also the state that the code runs with, i.e. data and/or external services, is changing. Each environment has its own state. System monitoring plays an important role here as it enables the team to identify the problems fast, so that the fixing can start as soon as possible. This is in favor of the time to restore service metric of DORA [2] or similarly mid time to identify (MTTI) metric.

---

[2]https://cloud.google.com/blog/products/devops-sre/using-the-four-keys-to-measure-your-devops-performance

Both of them play an important role in the performance of the system in place. Please check Identifying and Visualizing Risks.

When it comes to production, at least a certain level of monitoring must be in place. This includes but is not limited to system health checks and major functional tests, checking the key features of the product. On top of that, a more grained level of monitoring, i.e. response times with warning alarms should be active. However, the alarms should be fired only when it can make the team feel that "There is a problem and we have to look at it immediately."

So, keep the alarms meaningful and limited.

Indeed, there are numerous monitoring tools available, for instance Kibana, Grafana, Splunk etc. Getting into details however is far beyond the scope of this book. Your responsibility is to make sure that your system is monitored and actions are taken when the applications are not working as expected. Tools are helping here.

When firing an alarm, focus on the value. If alarms are to be ignored by the team because it is not very important, it means it is noise. Consider removing these alarms or explain its value if it is not well understood.

Technical Debt

Technical debt is an effort that is postponed to after delivery of a feature due to time constraints. This could be for instance refactoring, architectural changes or upgrade of a system etc. Indeed, teams can win some quick speed for certain deliveries, but in the long run an unmanageable technical debt hinders the team from delivering features fast and blocks the performance of the team. [3]

Technical debt as a whole is one of the most debatable topics between developers and Business Stakeholders. You are, however, responsible for providing the transparency, necessary guidance, and argumentation to your stakeholders so that the tech debt stays on a reasonable level. These questions could help:

- How far should you go in fine tuning a code base?
- How behind should you fall in upgrading a tech stack etc?
- What is the cost of delay for the debt?

I have experienced that it is pretty hard to find a way to avoid technical debt completely. However, it should be watched closely and kept at a reasonable level. This requires certain negotiation

---

[3]https://martinfowler.com/articles/is-quality-worth-cost.html

skills as well in order to provide necessary argumentation and make the risks transparent for relevant capacity planning.

Martin Fowler does not refer to technical debt as one unit, rather divides it into four quadrants [33]. Namely, reckless vs prudent and deliberate vs inadvertent. To elaborate it a bit more, here are different quadrants for technical debt:

1. **Prudent and deliberate:** You take a decision to deliver over making a good design, you want to solve your debt afterwards and keep an eye on that

2. **Reckless and deliberate:** You know well that your solution is bringing debt, but you are not interested in solving it at all, you go quick and dirty and ignore the consequences

3. **Prudent and inadvertent:** Sometimes you realize that a choice you made in the past was not the best for the given problem, but you did not know it before

4. **Reckless and inadvertent:** You are increasing your debt, but you are not even aware of that

---

[33]https://www.martinfowler.com/bliki/TechnicalDebtQuadrant.html

Now I would like to call you for action, write down one example you remember for each quadrant above listed:

1:_____
_____
_____
_____

2:_____
_____
_____
_____

3:_____
_____
_____
_____

4:_____
_____
_____
_____

Keep your business stakeholders up to date about the technical debt. If there is a case that slows down the delivery due to technical debt, make it pretty visible. Try to give numbers, especially on the effort lost due as much as possible.

Architecture Decision Records (ADRs)

Goal	Knowledge distribution
	Evolutionary architecture
Supports team dynamic(s)	Dependability
Opposes team dysfunction(s)	Avoidance of accountability

The team, product and system are in constant change and sometimes we may even forget the decisions and motivations behind. Here comes a solution for this problem; saving all the critical architectural decisions and their reasons, so that we can keep this information. This could bring the following advantages:

- A diary for the architecture itself
- A summary to show during onboarding new joiners, helps for knowledge sharing
- A proof how the architecture evolves and reasoning behind

There is no specific format or rule on how to do that, but the records could somehow show the date/time, decision, change, impact, risks etc...

Again, here the point is not to bring extra work to the team, rather to serve for the motivations above. Please do not overengineer but use it wisely! And it is up to the team what makes sense to put and what not.

💡 Check out the template for a better overview of a common ADR approach [29]

[29https://adr.github.io/

Goal	Building trust
	Limiting unknowns
	Transparency
Supports team dynamic(s)	Psychological safety
Opposes team dysfunction(s)	Avoidance of accountability
	Inattention to results

Security topic is a big topic that requires its own attention such as a separate book, but I could not skip it without mentioning it here to cover some essential points that you can deep dive afterwards.

We all know, there is no 100% secure system. Every system can be somehow compromised. However, security is a very essential aspect of software development and the Tech Lead is not only accountable to ensure the system's security to a certain extent but also to know what could go wrong and how to deal with them. Some of the basic rules every Tech Lead should ensure during development in the team:

- Zero trust principle which states that no one is being trusted by default from inside or outside the system
- Minimum access authorization
- Multi factor authentications are in place
- No passwords, credentials or tokens are committed to a repository
- Applying principles such as data is encrypted at rest and in motion
- Knowing what to do when an incident happens, simply incident handling

If there are any security guidelines in the organization, Tech Lead is responsible for ensuring implementation of these guidelines in the team together with all members.

Stated in the beginning, it is not possible to make any system 100% secure. However, to understand what could go wrong and its impact on the business as a whole, the team should be aware of the assets, the vulnerabilities and their impact.

As a Tech Lead, it could be sometimes hard to convince your stakeholders about implementing or enhancing security when there is some delivery pressure. Therefore, it is important to prioritize critical points and relevant capacity is being reserved. To understand that, a threat modeling workshop could be pretty useful. This helps the team to understand their assets, the potential vulnerabilities, their impact and how to tackle them.

There are several tools and methods that you can find on the web on how to drive that. One approach could be:

- Understanding and listing all the assets (i.e. database, APIs, services, data, users etc)
- Listing all potential scenarios & vulnerabilities
- Creating an importance & likelihood map
- The more important the asset and likely the incident is, the higher the risk is!
- Create counter actions to mitigate the risk
- Prioritize them based on the risk
- Create actions for each risk

Once you have actions prioritized, you can then start to implement them already. This will also help to make all the security risks visible to your stakeholders, which in return contributes to trust and transparency aspects.

Here is an example of how it could look like.

Importance of asset

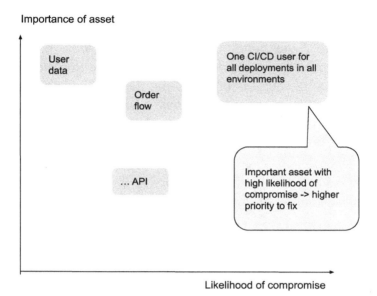

Figure 3: A sample risk map after threat modeling

I have experienced that these workshops are not bringing something new or unknown, but rather making them more transparent and helped me to convince my stakeholders to separate capacity for implementing the necessary fixes. However, it also gave team members a better understanding of security and its importance.

Penetration Testing

Consider having a preferably independent party to do some security checks on your APIs, applications etc. It is better to work on leakages before somebody else finds it out. This costs some money for sure, but it is all about the risk and its impact if you would not do it. In this case, the impact and harm could be much higher than the cost invested for testing.

Goal	Building trust
	Limiting unknowns
	Transparency
Supports team dynamic(s)	Psychological safety
Opposes team dysfunction(s)	Avoidance of accountability
	Inattention to results

In the beginning of my career, I was focusing on creating systems that would never fail. This was my ultimate goal. In time I understood that I was aiming for perfection which was not possible. My focus shifted from perfection to good enough for requirements, which was more realistic, doable and simpler.

Based on your business requirements, you may need to build a very resilient system. We all know that failures are inevitable. That said, it is important to understand how your system would behave when something goes wrong and you can take necessary actions accordingly to cover some scenarios and make your system more resilient. Here comes chaos engineering as a good method.

Chaos engineering is basically simulation of unexpected system failures to test a system's behavior and recovery plan. [32] Based on the results, you can learn what could be improved and take necessary actions afterwards.

[32]https://www.thoughtworks.com/en-in/insights/blog/agile-engineering-practices
/building-resiliency-chaos-engineering

How to Run?

Consider doing a hacking day, where your team divides into two groups. Team A destroys some services (i.e. in the staging environment) or the whole environment and Team B is responsible to bring it back. You can have a good opportunity here to understand:

- **Identification time:** How long does it take till your team realizes that there is a problem. (Mid time to identify - MTTI)

- **Recovery time:** How long does it take to reinstall the environment, or fixing the bug. Remember that it is one of the DORA metrics [2]

- **Team spirit:** How good your team is working on problems together

- **Team confidence:** A great learning opportunity and team members can gain confidence, making them feel more comfortable to deliver; because even if there are failures, they can learn to fix them fast

---

[2]https://cloud.google.com/blog/products/devops-sre/using-the-four-keys-to-mea sure-your-devops-performance

Goal	Customer satisfaction
	Automation
	Faster and frequent delivery
	Visible progress
	Agility
Supports team dynamic(s)	Impact
Opposes team dysfunction(s)	Inattention to results

So, now we have visited many practices that indeed help to reach the continuous delivery capability. Now we can talk about the main aspect of technical excellence; the continuous delivery. Indeed, continuous delivery is a pretty big and important topic. However, I am happy to cover the basics and certain arguments to explain why and how it can be done.

Living in a fast changing world, it is crucial to serve the needs of the end user in a timely manner and react to their feedback. That also means, to adapt to change faster and easier, core of agility. Of course it depends on the product, but having cycles of two weeks for fixing a bug or releasing a feature was not fitting into our goals anymore for having a high customer satisfaction and frequent feedback.

Continuous delivery comes here as a solution to avoid waiting time and immediately deliver the value to the end user when applicable. Therefore, we triggered the change, not only the product, tools and technologies behind, but also the way of delivering value.

I would like to start with some definitions to make it clear what we are talking about. [15], [16]

- **Continuous integration:** This is about frequently integrating the local development codebase into the trunk or so called main branch

- **Continuous delivery:** Being capable of deploying the latest codebase whenever requested. This means, the codebase on the main branch is always up to date and ready to deploy, but usually it is upon a decision when to deploy to the production environment

[15]https://martinfowler.com/articles/continuousIntegration.html
[16]https://martinfowler.com/bliki/ContinuousDelivery.html

- **Continuous deployment:** Every integration into the main branch goes into production without any prior request. From a developer perspective, any push to origin repository of the main branch is expected to be deployed automatically into production (assuming it passes all the quality gates such as automated tests)

Indeed, continuous delivery may have certain resistance from your stakeholders or even developers. Some argumentations below I have witnessed so far.

Counter Argumentation

What I heard mostly in the beginning of the project(s) could be listed through:

- This is very dangerous
- Our developers make mistakes. We have to control it
- We can not do that

and similar arguments.

Now, let's move forward to sharing what we applied to achieve continuous deployment.

As continuous delivery is tightly connected to technical excellence and high performance teams, I am happy to share my experience on how I convinced my team members coming from different backgrounds and stakeholders to apply continuous delivery.

Seeding the Idea and Internal Trainings

In order to do such a change, it is essential to make people familiar with the idea by talking about what the alternatives can be. I have encouraged developers and together we have conducted several agile principles and development practices sessions where we talked and aligned on certain development principles within team(s). This also includes how continuous deployment could serve for many agile principles such as frequent delivery, measure progress, welcome the change etc.

Meanwhile, we took actions and applied certain automation on our deployment pipeline. Now it is time to take a step back and look at the overall picture.

To illustrate the steps of development and deployment a bit better, below is a pipeline.

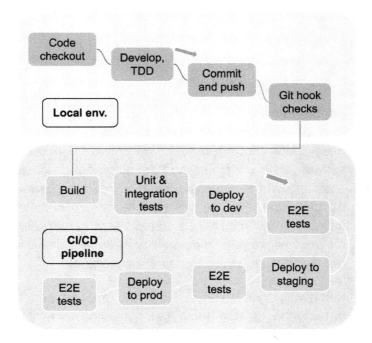

Figure 4: CI/CD pipeline without failures

A mature pipeline with certain test coverage is more likely to catch and mitigate errors.In a success scenario, the tests and all the checks will be green in the pipeline as depicted above.

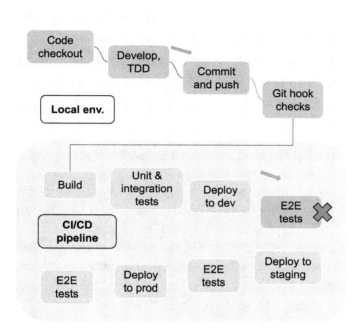

Figure 5: CI/CD pipeline with failures

On the other hand, one step failing will prevent the code from going further in the pipeline. I.e end to end tests on the development environment. This is possible thanks to good test coverage.

Since the development is already done incrementally in small steps and it takes minutes to deploy to production, the fix is likely to be a small one and fast to deploy.

Summary

Technical excellence is strongly related to the continuous delivery capabilities of a team. In order to reach this maturity level, there has to be many practices in place, such as automated testing, good test coverage, pair programming, trunk based development, ensuring quality and more.

Despite all these practices, there will still be errors. However, the focus here is not to avoid failures completely, but to fix them very fast. Thanks to several practices the failures will likely be fixed through automated deployments without waiting times such as code reviews. Moreover, the progress in the development will be more visible with the help of incremental changes and frequent deployments, which makes the changes small and so, easier to fix.

There are likely already organizational practices on how to deliver software. These practices mentioned here are a guideline and provide a perspective on how it could be done. Indeed, I have provided some practices and methods that worked for me pretty well during my projects. Of course, these can vary based on different products as well as organizations.

133

Value

Third Pillar: Value

"Our highest priority is to satisfy the customer through the early and continuous delivery of valuable software." [1]

Does the above statement sound familiar? It is the first one listed in the 12 agile principles.

When developing a feature or software; *"How will this impact the value we deliver to our customer ?"* is one of the fundamental questions leaders should ask. [17]

In value based thinking, you don't focus on increasing your revenue, rather you focus on delivering value to the customer and expect that your revenue will follow afterwards. [17] In other words, you always focus on the customer value when you develop software. [18]

Agile principles clearly state that we need to focus on the customer's value. As a Tech Lead, you are driving customer value oriented thinking in the team and helping developers to find a valuable reason on everything they are building.

---

[1]https://agilemanifesto.org/principles.html
[17]https://www.thoughtworks.com/en-de/insights/books/edge
[18]https://digital.ai/catalyst-blog/what-is-value-based-delivery-and-how-it-can-benefit-your-organization/

The impact could be direct through a user story or indirect through an enablement story, where for instance some tech debt is optimized, technical enablement is done or technology stack is upgraded. Even in the indirect cases, there should be outcomes that are affecting the value in a positive aspect. For instance, implementing automated testing and meaningful coverage is to make sure that a feature is delivered to customers faster.

That said, one of the worst things that can happen is when the team is doing great engineering implementations but bringing little to no value to the customers. In this case, the team is still low performing no matter how well they are writing code, how frequently they are deploying etc. In the end, it is the value delivered that counts. Therefore the value focus is as important as the technical excellence and leadership aspects of effective technical leadership. In this section, namely the third pillar of an effective technical leadership we will dive into several features on how to focus on the value during software development and delivery.

Without heavily diving into the big landscape of the business, Tech Leads should be capable of driving certain aspects of value driven development and delivery in the team. In order to achieve that, the Tech Lead keeps better these questions in mind:

- How will an effort impact the value we deliver to our customers?
- How well is this feature fitting into strategic goals?
- Is there a clear acceptance criteria, definition of done and scope? (covered in the next chapters)
- What is the cost of delay of a particular feature, bug fix etc?
- How focused is the team or in other words, how many tasks run in parallel, work In progress (WIP)?

Please note that this section is written more of an assumption that your customers are end users of products you are building. In a different case i.e when you are a consultant and supporting a client to build a product, there the value focus would be more of delivering the capabilities which your client is trying to implement, because your customer is actually your client. As a summary, the key point here is focusing on your customer needs.

Goal	Aligning with the organizational goals
Supports team dynamic(s)	Meaning Impact
Opposes team dysfunction(s)	Inattention to results

An effective Tech Lead could foresee the impact of the upcoming features on the technology choices, tools and assets. For instance, if a solution is to be provided to customers worldwide, you need to take that into account in your architecture. That does not mean that you build a very complex system for MVP, but rather you know what will come up in the future.

More questions to take into account on your journey:

- What is the vision of the company?
- How is that translated into strategic goals and how does your team, project or product fit in generally?

- Who are your targeted users and what problem(s) are you trying to solve with your application, software or tool?
- What is the road map for the software you are building and where are you right now?
- How could all these affect your technological decision?

A value focused effective technical leadership is to make sure that the technological solutions are serving customer value. That is why you need to work very closely on a daily basis with business stakeholders such as the Product Owner. These roles have different names in different organizations but in general we are talking here about Product Owners, Product Managers, Business Owners etc.

The challenge increases here when the organizational strategic goals are not customer value driven, but more internally driven. In this context, it could be hard for you to drive a value driven approach, as it may not fit into organization goals directly. What you could do here as a Tech Lead is to ask value oriented questions as above to increase awareness for a value driven approach. Either way, working closely with your business stakeholders could help to find a good way to move forward.

Goal	Business value
	Customer satisfaction
	Aligning with the organizational goals
Supports team dynamic(s)	Meaning
	Impact
Opposes team dysfunction(s)	Inattention to results

Here comes the fun part, because as the Tech Lead, you are somehow representing the development part of the team. However, you are also accountable for delivering the requirements and bringing the most value by making your team perform high.

It is here pretty crucial to have strong communication and often multiple interactions on daily bases with your business counter partner (i.e. Product Owner) This is also in line with the agile principle where it states "Business people and developers must work together daily throughout the project." [1]

The relationship between the business stakeholders and the Tech Lead is so important that, without a good working one, we can not make it confidently sure whether the team is actually delivering value. Because, even if the team can make awesome technical progress, it does not necessarily mean that they are performing high. A high performance team includes the amount of value the team is bringing, and the value is to be aligned together with your business stakeholders.

Please note that the business representative in the team is just another member of the team. That means, I recommend that the Product Owner and developers are just in contact with each other without the Tech Lead having to be in between. This creates a more natural environment and helps developers to understand the business value faster.

---

[1]https://agilemanifesto.org/principles.html

For instance, when you want to consider solving some tech debt, talk to your business stakeholder and explain what it brings, what problem it solves and let them challenge you.

Another example could be, make them become aware of the risks, this could be delivery as well as security risks. Have an aligned and informed decision on what that means.

So, be transparent, include your business stakeholder in decision making, find priorities together and enjoy!

Never forget that, it is not development vs business, you are ONE team and everyone's opinion matters. When it is hard to come to a decision, remember the goal of the team and try to bring the conversation into how you all work for the common goal, remind it to yourself and the team.

Continuous Product Discovery

Goal	Business value
	Customer satisfaction
	Aligning with the organizational goals
Supports team dynamic(s)	Meaning
	Impact
Opposes team dysfunction(s)	Inattention to results

Continuous discovery is a method of user research employed by agile teams, involving ongoing and small-scale research activities throughout the entire product development process. This ensures that customer feedback is integrated into every product decision as opposed to relying on a single research event at the project's outset. [23]

[23]https://www.interaction-design.org/literature/topics/continuous-discovery

This sounds familiar right?

Indeed; continuous discovery really looks like the counterpart of continuous delivery in the product context. Instead of defining the product in the beginning, there should be constant discovery of the product based on the customer feedback and needs. [22]

Customer feedback can be collected in many ways. Direct input, feedback forms and contact are only some ways. Monitoring their behaviors and collecting relevant data to understand their needs, pain points and what they would like to have is yet another approach.

The continuous discovery or in general Product Discovery falls in the expertise of your business stakeholder. This is mostly and often driven by Product Owner and Designers. However, a technical aspect is necessary to make sure that the expectations are realistic and could be planned reasonably as well. Therefore it is crucial that you work closely and support your product owner and/or designer on the discovery to avoid any loss of effort.

---

[22]https://www.agile-academy.com/de/product-owner/continuous-discovery/

Goal	Aligning with the organizational goals Business value Customer satisfaction
Supports team dynamic(s)	Structure and clarity Meaning Impact
Opposes team dysfunction(s)	Inattention to results

As the Tech Lead is accountable for the performance of the team, and performance of the team is strongly connected to the value the team brings, it becomes crucial what is delivered in which order, because this is what the team is supposed to deliver.

Planning and prioritization should be tightly connected to business needs. What you can contribute here as a Tech Lead is to work together with your business stakeholder(s) and provide transparency in order to make the work and progress more visible, doable and smooth.

If Scrum is in place, in the ideal case you want your tickets with size that all of them are completed within a sprint, that it is deployable and the value is contributed to the end user.

Questions to keep in mind here:

- Are your tasks strongly aligned with business goals?
- Are you making sure that we are prioritizing the high value for the end user?
- The cost of delay for certain tasks?
- Is there overengineering or tech debt?
- Can things be done simpler?
- How big are the tickets?
- Can one pair finish the ticket on their own in one sprint?
- How often are tickets spread over more than one sprint?

💡 You are expected to understand and sometimes challenge business decisions as well, give your input but once an agreement is in place, fully commit to it.

💡 Do not limit the discussions between the business stakeholders and development to yourself. Let the developers speak their minds, contribute and learn how to contribute to planning and prioritization as well. Help them grow by taking them out of their comfort zone in between.

Definitions of Done (DoD) and Acceptance Criteria

Goal	Increasing delivery speed Limiting unknowns
Supports team dynamic(s)	Structure and clarity Impact
Opposes team dysfunction(s)	Inattention to results

Have you experienced or witnessed non-ending tasks? A task that was supposed to take 2 weeks but already 5 weeks gone and still ongoing? This happens unfortunately in between and there are some methods to avoid that.

Creating tasks (or tickets) in small iterable chunks is absolutely one part of the solution. However, not less important is basically to put clear boundaries and expectations from a ticket. Here come the acceptance criteria and definition of done in place for help.

Although they look similar, they serve slightly different purposes. Acceptance criteria are functional requirements from a ticket (or a feature) [20], literally listing what the end effect from a user point of view should be so that the relevant requirement is met. On the other hand, definition of done focuses on the big picture such as quality aspects, testing, documentation, security and integration etc. These are not tied to a specific user story but a general aspect of delivery, it is a broader approach. [21]

Acceptance criteria are either met or not met. Likewise, the definition of done can also be either done or not done. There is no state in between!

I would strongly recommend having both and having "All acceptance criteria are met" as one criteria in the definition of done.

---

[20]https://resources.scrumalliance.org/Article/need-know-acceptance-criteria
[21]https://resources.scrumalliance.org/Article/definition-dod

Goal	Building trust
	Limiting unknowns
	Transparency
Supports team dynamic(s)	Structure and clarity
	Impact
Opposes team dysfunction(s)	Inattention to results

The projects are running, development is in progress but there are some risks on delivery. It is your responsibility to see, identify and make them visible to your stakeholders.

Your potential questions which should be in your radar are:

- Is the delivery at risk?
- Are there potential security issues?
- How is the tech debt?
- What is your approach for mitigating the risk?

It is not easy to have answers to all of these questions, but you are responsible for making them visible first. Transparency is an important parameter for building trust. Depending on the risk itself, there could be different people involved in decision making, including some members outside the team. Tech Lead's main responsibility here is to inform and involve the relevant people for the risks, and find a way to deal with them.

💡 Suppose that you have a road map but it looks like you are behind the schedule. Better not to wait until the last moment, but connect to your stakeholders, explain the situation and work with them to do a re-prioritisation. Consider listing the tasks as must have, should have and nice to have. This way, you deliver the most value possible, even though not all desired features can be delivered.

Goal	Using technology as a tool
Supports team dynamic(s)	Impact
Opposes team dysfunction(s)	Inattention to results

As a Tech Lead, your responsibility is to make sure that the technology you are building is serving value. That means, whatever the team is implementing, it should somehow contribute to this goal: Bringing customer value.

Who cares if you build something with super cool technologies but it brings no value or no one is happy using it?

It is indeed, one of your core duties to explain and convince the developers to focus on the value during their daily work.

From my experience and observations, it is not difficult for developers to fall into a trap, aiming for cool technologies but forgetting the focus on the value behind, sometimes even enforcing a solution driven by "cool technologies" before solid discussions in the problem space.

I often hear this sentence, "We use cool technologies". Developers are happy to do so and depending on the teams and the projects, these can range from programming languages to tools, platforms, development environments, libraries and so on. In my opinion, it could bring the following advantages:

- Increasing the motivation of developers
- In general they are modern and up to date
- Easier to attract talents. i.e. hiring process.

On the other hand, it may hold some downsides such as:

- Overtaking the focus on the value
- Over complication of tooling, technologies or architecture
- Being unknown by the most of the team
- Immaturity or Instability

That said, I am afraid that they can become the actual goal instead of a tool for reaching your team's goals.

Just as a reminder, the team's goal is to bring value. This value is often related to the end user in product teams, but in general defined by the organization, team, product and/or the business. Increasing the end user satisfaction is one example, bringing the features to the end users faster could be just another one. The development capacity is limited, and it is important to make a valuable prioritization. Asking the questions below helps to find out what makes best sense:

- What's the easiest and fastest way to solve this exact problem?
- What do we know is on the short and mid term road map of features that might have an impact on technology decisions?
- Who else is relying on our technology decision, will they be able to use it/ learn it/ maintain it?

That also means, if you can solve your problem in a simple way and architecture, consider just keeping it simple. If it is bringing value, go for it. Just make sure that your solutioning is actually serving business value.

Cool Technologies or Technical Excellence

Please note that cool technologies are something different than technical excellence. I have talked about this part in the technical excellence pillar. As said, Martin Fowler relates technical excellence more with continuous delivery [4]. All these are somehow also co-related to non-functional requirements such as maintainability, observability and so on.

To summarize, there is nothing wrong with using cool technologies, as long as they are serving high value to the end user.

---

[4]https://www.youtube.com/watch?v=Avs70dZ3Vlk

157

Summary

In the value pillar, I provided you with relevant methods to foster value based thinking and value focus in your team. The team builds solutions for bringing value. The value is to be defined and aligned together with your business stakeholders which should be in line with organizational goals and strategy. Remember that, technical excellence is related to continuous delivery and continuous delivery is about delivering value to the customer.

I would like to finish this section by the agile principle:

"Our highest priority is to satisfy the customer through the early and continuous delivery of valuable software." [1]

---

[1]https://agilemanifesto.org/principles.html

Potential
Role
Distributions

Potential Role Distributions

I have experienced several setups to cover these responsibilities for effective technical leadership in teams. As we covered the three pillars already, it is worth visiting some common setups for giving more insights. It is beyond the scope of this book to cover all the different role combinations, but I hope it will give you an idea on potential common combinations. There is no universally accepted setup, rather these change from organization to organization.

In some organizations, there are Tech Leads covering all the responsibilities listed in the three pillars. They focus not only on the technology but also leadership and ensuring value bringing. In this setup, there is also a Product representative such as Product Owner. A sample set up of a cross functional team may look like below:

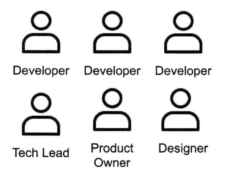

Developer   Developer   Developer

Tech Lead   Product   Designer
             Owner

Figure 6: Team setup without an Engineering Manager

A sample setup above and this could work in small teams efficiently due to limited complexity, but can be overwhelming for the tech lead in big teams. There comes some other roles into play to take over some responsibilities to make it more sustainable for the individuals leading the team.

In different organizations this role can be called differently, such as Lead Developer, Lead Engineer, Technical Lead, Engineering Manager, Engineering Lead, Tech Designer, Staff Engineer etc.

In this book, we assumed that the setup above shown in Figure 6 is the setup for a particular team we are talking about, where Tech Lead handles all the responsibilities mentioned in the book.

Team Setup with an Engineering Manager and a Lead Developer

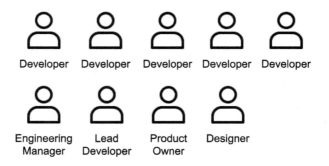

Figure 7: Team setup with an Engineering Manager

Within this combination, the responsibilities of effective technical leadership are shared among an Engineering Manager and a Lead Developer (or sometimes called Tech Lead). While the Lead Developer can focus more on technical topics such as technical excellence, value delivery, architecture, while the Engineering Manager takes over the responsibilities covering the management and organizational duties such as peoples growth, performance assessments, team health, vacation planning, working closely with the business stakeholders and more.

As an advantage here, the Lead Developer can have more time and focus for technical excellence while all the organizational tasks are delegated to the Engineering Manager. On the other hand, the Lead Developer should still keep value focus in mind and mentor other developers, which will be also part of Engineering Manager's responsibility to remind and keep all developers focused on value.

This setup is particularly applicable when teams are big enough (i.e. 8-12 people), so that the Lead Developer is not overloaded and has enough time for driving technical topics.

Team Setup with a Senior Engineering Manager and Tech Lead(s)

In this setup, an Engineering Manager is responsible for managing more than one team, and each team still has a Tech Lead. The Tech Lead takes a bit more responsibility than the case above because the Engineering Manager has less time per team and their members. This is up to the team and organization on deciding what is covered by whom. In general, performance assessments, business stakeholder management, bridging between business and development are still covered by the Engineering Manager, while the remaining is by the Tech Lead such as technical excellence, knowledge distribution and even growing other team members technically.

Summary

I believe that effective technical leadership is creating effective teams that are leading for success. There are certain tasks and methods a leader can drive so that the team becomes effective and successful.

In this section, we covered some of the common setups in different organizations, where the responsibilities of the Technical Leadership is distributed over different roles. The book is actually covering these responsibilities in three pillars into one role, namely Tech Lead.

Reverse Mapping
of
Methods

Reverse Mapping of Methods

As there are several methods and we have examined their impact on team dynamics and Dysfunctions, it is worth putting them all together, so that you can navigate and find out methods based on the map easily. Each entry in the map is arguably set. That means, it is up to you to add or remove, or whatever pick up based on your use case.

The Team Dynamics and Contributing Methods Map

This map summarizes the methods that could be used to enhance the relevant team dynamic.

Team Dynamic to Enhance	Method to apply
Psychological safety	Listen
	No Finger Pointing
	Creating Safe Environment
	Driving Challenging Technical Discussions
	1on1s
	Reading Between Lines
	Team Health Checks
	Security and Threat Modeling
	Preparation for Failures: Chaos Engineering

Dependability	Enabling, Empowering and Delegation
	1on1s
	Team Health Checks
	Knowledge Distribution
	Pair Programming
	Testing: Why It Matters
Structure and clarity	Foster Communication
	Roles and Responsibilities
	Core Values and Ways of Working
	Planning & Prioritisation
	Identifying and Visualizing Risks
Meaning	Involve In Decision Making
	Core Values and Ways of Working
	Understanding the Value and Strategic Goals
	Working With a Product

	Owner
	Continuous Product Discovery
	Planning & Prioritisation
Impact	Involve in Decision Making
	Do Not Micromanage
	Letting Your Team Members Shine
	Team Health Checks
	Pair Programming
	Test Driven Development and Automated Testing
	Trunk Based Development
	System Monitoring
	Continuous Integration / Continuous Delivery
	Understanding the Value and Strategic Goals
	Working With a Product Owner/Manager

	Continuous Product Discovery
	Planning & Prioritisation
	Definitions of Done (DOD) and Acceptance Criteria
	Identifying and Visualizing Risks
	Tech Lead's Challenge With Cool Technologies

The Five Dysfunctions and Opposing Methods Map

Similarly, below is a map for the Five Dysfunctions and methods to apply for opposing them.

The Dysfunctions to Oppose	Method to apply
Absence of trust	Listen
	No Finger Pointing
	Foster Communication
	Creating Safe Environment
	Letting Your Team Members Shine
	1on1s
	Feedback Culture
	Reading Between Lines
	Team Health Checks
	Onboarding / Offboarding
	Knowledge Distribution

	Tech Huddles
Fear of conflict	Creating Safe Environment
	Driving Challenging Technical Discussions
	Feedback Culture
	Reading Between Lines
	Tech Huddles
	Pair Programming
	Team Health Checks
Lack of commitment	Involve in Decision Making
	Do not Micromanage
	Team Health Checks
	Roles and Responsibilities
	Tech Huddles
Avoidance of accountability	Roles and Responsibilities
	Core Values and Ways of

	working
	Architecture Decision Records (ADRs)
	Security and Threat Modeling
	Preparation for Failures: Chaos Engineering
Inattention to results	Involve in Decision Making
	Do not Micromanage
	Core Values and Ways of working
	Testing: Why It matters
	System Monitoring
	Continuous Integration / Continuous Delivery
	Security and Threat Modeling
	Preparation for Failures: Chaos Engineering

	Understanding the Value and Strategic Goals
	Working with a Product Owner
	Continuous Product Discovery
	Planning & Prioritisation
	Definitions of Done (DoD) and Acceptance Criteria
	Identifying and Visualizing Risks
	Tech Lead's Challenge with Cool Technologies

Closing Words

In this book, I shared the perspectives, practices and methods I learned and applied during my journey as a Tech Lead for many years.

Effective technical leadership is not a target, rather it is a journey. You learn in time, you practice it, sometimes you succeed, sometimes you fail. You are not perfect and it is OK! What is important is to continuously learn from your failures and apply them in your next challenge.

You can be very passionate about the title, but actually it happens on its own. My observation for most of the successful Tech Leads is that, they already demonstrate their leadership skills and at some point they are recognised by the organization and the title changes.

As a summary, lead by example!
Be the leader you wanted when you were less experienced. (citation unknown)

I hope you enjoyed reading the book and it is worth the time you spent.

Bests,
Mesut Ayata

References

[1] Agile Principles from Agile Manifesto,
https://agilemanifesto.org/principles.html

[2] DORA Metrics by Dora Team / Google,
https://cloud.google.com/blog/products/devops-sre/using-the-four-keys-to-measure-your-devops-performance

[3] Is High Quality Software Worth the Cost? by Martin Fowler,
https://martinfowler.com/articles/is-quality-worth-cost.html

[4] What Does Tech Excellence Look Like? by Martin Fowler,
https://www.youtube.com/watch?v=Avs70dZ3Vlk

[5] The Five Dysfunctions of a Team by Lencioni

[6] Test Driven Development by Torczuk,
https://www.thoughtworks.com/insights/blog/test-driven-development-best-thing-has-happened-software-design

[7] Building Evolutionary Architectures by Ford, Parsons and Kua,
https://www.thoughtworks.com/en-de/insights/books/building-evolutionary-architectures

[8] Prime Directive by Kerth,
https://www.thoughtworks.com/en-de/insights/blog/applying-prime-directive-beyond-retrospective

[9] Active Listening by Leading Effectively Stuff,
https://www.ccl.org/articles/leading-effectively-articles/coaching-others-use-active-listening-skills/

[10] What speedback is ... by Gomes and Hoffman,
https://www.thoughtworks.com/en-de/insights/blog/what-speedback-and-how-run-it-using-zoom-breakout-rooms

[11] Trunk Based Development by Naik,
https://www.thoughtworks.com/en-de/insights/blog/enabling-trunk-based-development-deployment-pipelines

[12] Managing Feature Toggles by Börding and Upton,
https://www.thoughtworks.com/en-de/insights/blog/managing-feature-to
ggles-teams

[13] What is Pair Programming by Gillis,
https://www.techtarget.com/searchsoftwarequality/definition/Pair-progra
mming

[14] Seven Principles of Pair Programming Etiquette by Qiu,
https://www.thoughtworks.com/en-de/insights/blog/seven-principles-pai
r-programming-etiquette

[15] Continuous Integration by Martin Fowler,
https://martinfowler.com/articles/continuousIntegration.html

[16] Continuous Delivery by Martin Fowler,
https://martinfowler.com/bliki/ContinuousDelivery.html

[17] EDGE - Value Driven Digital Transformation by Highsmith, Luu
and Robinson,
https://www.thoughtworks.com/en-de/insights/books/edge

[18] What is Value Based Delivery... by Rabinovitz,
https://digital.ai/catalyst-blog/what-is-value-based-delivery-and-how-it-c
an-benefit-your-organization/

[19] Exploring Value-Oriented Incremental Delivery by Santhanam,
https://www.thoughtworks.com/en-de/insights/blog/exploring-value-orie
nted-incremental-delivery

[20] Acceptance Criteria by Scrum Alliance,
https://resources.scrumalliance.org/Article/need-know-acceptance-crite
ria

[21] Definition of Done by Panchal,
https://resources.scrumalliance.org/Article/definition-dod

[22] Continuous Discovery in Scrum by Salimi,
https://www.agile-academy.com/de/product-owner/continuous-discover
y/

[23] Continuous Discovery by Klein,
https://www.interaction-design.org/literature/topics/continuous-discover
y

[24] Getting Started with Github Co-Pilot by Boeckeler,
https://www.thoughtworks.com/en-de/insights/blog/generative-ai/getting
-started-with-github-copilot

[25] Oxford Learners Dictionary by Oxford University Press

[26] Five Dynamics of an Effective Team by Google,
https://www.thinkwithgoogle.com/intl/en-emea/consumer-insights/cons
umer-trends/five-dynamics-effective-team/

[27] Take the DORA Quick Check by Dora Team / Google,
https://dora.dev/quickcheck/

[28] The Culture Map by Erin Meyer,
https://erinmeyer.com/books/the-culture-map/

[29] Architecture Decision Records by ADR GitHub organization,
https://adr.github.io/

[30] What is a sprint retrospective by Scrum.org
https://www.scrum.org/resources/what-is-a-sprint-retrospective

[31] How to conduct a successful sprint retrospective by Atlassian,
https://www.atlassian.com/team-playbook/plays/retrospective

[32] Building resiliency with chaos engineering by Parekh and
Ramakrishnan,
https://www.thoughtworks.com/en-in/insights/blog/agile-engineering-pr
actices/building-resiliency-chaos-engineering

[33] Technical Debt Quadrant by Martin Fowler,
https://www.martinfowler.com/bliki/TechnicalDebtQuadrant.html

[34] PIT Mutation Testing, https://pitest.org/

[35] What is Mutation Testing by Gillis,
https://www.techtarget.com/searchitoperations/definition/mutation-testi
ng

[36] Thoughtworks Technology Radar,
https://www.thoughtworks.com/radar

[37] What is Consumer Driven Contract Testing by pact,
https://pactflow.io/what-is-consumer-driven-contract-testing/

[38] Consumer-Driven Contracts: A Service Evolution Pattern by
Robinson,
https://martinfowler.com/articles/consumerDrivenContracts.html

[39] The Practical Test Pyramid by Vocke,
https://martinfowler.com/articles/practical-test-pyramid.html

[40] Software Testing Guide by Fowler, https://martinfowler.com/testing/

Figures

Figure 1: The Three Pillars of Effective Technical Leadership in The Three Pillars

Figure 2: A draft roles and responsibilities workshop outcome in Roles and Responsibilities

Figure 3: A sample risk map after threat modeling in Security and Threat Modeling

Figure 4: CI/CD pipeline without failures in Continuous Delivery

Figure 5: CI/CD pipeline with failures in Continuous Delivery

Figure 6: Team setup without an Engineering Manager in Potential Role Distributions

Figure 7: Team setup with an Engineering Manager in Potential Role Distributions

Pictures

[1] High Performance Team by fauxels,
https://www.pexels.com/photo/photo-of-people-near-wooden-table-318
4418/

[2] Leadership by Padrinan,
https://www.pexels.com/photo/paper-boats-on-solid-surface-194094/

[3] Onboarding by Inacio,
https://www.pexels.com/photo/black-and-white-photo-of-people-boardin
g-an-underground-train-15848202/

[4] Pair Programming by Morillo,
https://www.pexels.com/photo/two-women-looking-at-the-code-at-lapto
p-1181263/

Icons

[1] Tip icon created by Pixel perfect - Flaticon,
 https://www.flaticon.com/free-icon/lamp_2910914

[2] Scenario icon created by Freepik - Flaticon,
https://www.flaticon.com/free-icon/screenplay_2178123